I0413216

Women's pathways to jail:
The roles & intersections of serious mental illness & trauma

Submitted by:

Shannon M. Lynch, Ph.D.
Idaho State University

Dana D. DeHart, Ph.D.
University of South Carolina

Joanne Belknap, Ph.D.
University of Colorado

Bonnie L. Green, Ph.D.
Georgetown University

September 2012

Submitted to the Bureau of Justice Assistance

Bureau of Justice Assistance
U.S. Department of Justice

This project was supported by Grant No. 2010-DB-BX-K048 awarded by the Bureau of Justice Assistance. The Bureau of Justice Assistance is a component of the Office of Justice Programs, which also includes the Bureau of Justice Statistics, the National Institute of Justice, the Office of Juvenile Justice and Delinquency Prevention, the Office for Victims of Crime, and the Office of Sex Offender Sentencing, Monitoring, Apprehending, Registering, and Tracking. Points of view or opinions in this document are those of the author and do not necessarily represent the official position or policies of the U.S. Department of Justice.

Acknowledgements

This project would not have been possible without the support of many jail staff and research team members at each site. We specifically want to recognize the contributions of research team members Kristine Johnson, Elizabeth Whalley and Priscilla Dass-Brailsford for their work on project coordination, interview training and/or interviewer supervision. In addition, our thanks to Jemima Anglade, Alina Bonci, Porschia Brown, Toyin Falebita, Pat Heiber, Kelsie Hendrickson, Ania Hornberger, Alejandra Hurtado, Beena Kuruvilla, Andrea Lamont, Kathrine Martinez, Anjali Nandi, Kathryn Nowotny, Sarah Rowland, Adriana Serrano, and Emily Van Ness for assistance interviewing and research contributions. We also give special thanks to the women who shared their stories and experiences with the hope of making a difference for those who will follow them.

ABSTRACT

This multi-site study addressed critical gaps in the literature by assessing the prevalence of serious mental illness (SMI), posttraumatic stress disorder (PTSD), and substance use disorders (SUD) in women in jail and pathways to offending for women with and without SMI. Using a randomly selected sample ($N = 491$) from rural and urban jails, this study employed a structured diagnostic interview to assess current and lifetime prevalence of SMI (e.g., major depression, bipolar, and psychotic spectrum disorders), PTSD, and SUD in women in jail. Women's prior access to treatment and level of functional impairment in the past 12 months was also assessed. Next, qualitative Life History Calendar (LHC) interviews were conducted with a subset of the sample ($N = 115$) to examine how onset of different types of criminal activity and delinquency vary as a function of mental health status and trauma exposure. Finally, we also interviewed corrections staff members ($N = 37$) at participating jail sites to assess staff members' perceptions about the prevalence of mental health difficulties in women in jail as well as staff beliefs about women's pathways to jail. Notably, 43% of participants met criteria for a lifetime SMI, and 32% met SMI criteria in the past 12 months. Substance use disorders were the most commonly occurring disorders, with 82% of the sample meeting lifetime criteria for drug or alcohol abuse or dependence. Similarly, PTSD rates were high with just over half the sample (53%) meeting criteria for lifetime PTSD. Women also met criteria for multiple lifetime disorders at high rates. Finally, 30 to 45% of individuals who met criteria for a current disorder reported severely impaired functioning in the past year. Women with SMI reported greater rates of victimization and more extensive offending histories than women who did not meet criteria for lifetime SMI. In a test of our proposed model, experiences of childhood victimization and adult trauma did not directly predict offending histories; instead both forms of victimization increased the risk of poor mental health, and poor mental health predicted a greater offending history. Next, quantitative LHC data were analyzed to elucidate patterns of offending over the lifespan. SMI significantly increased women's risk for onset of substance use, drug dealing/charges, property crime, fighting/assault, and running away. In addition, experiences of victimization predicted risk of offending. The third component of this study included interviews with corrections staff including supervisors, health practitioners, and corrections officers/deputies. These staff members indicated a general awareness that women's experiences of victimization were linked with their entry into the criminal justice system. Further, many staff were aware of women's mental health problems. In particular, they expressed concern that there were limited resources in jail for women struggling with mental illness, and that women were then released from jail with little to no assistance to support their attempts to change behavior and lifestyle. Understanding female offenders' pathways to offending, including both risk for onset and risk for continued offending, helps elucidate the complexity of their experiences and identify key factors and intervening variables that may ameliorate or exacerbate risk. This type of research is critical to development of gender responsive programming, alternatives to incarceration, and problem-solving court initiatives.

Executive Summary

INTRODUCTION

The rate of incarceration of women has increased substantially in recent decades, with a 31% increase between 2000 and 2011 (Minton, 2012). Female offenders appear to have different risk factors for offending than do male offenders. In particular, female offenders report greater incidence of mental health problems and serious mental illness than do male offenders (James & Glaze, 2006; Steadman, Osher, Robbins, Case, & Samuels, 2009) and higher rates of substance dependence as well as greater incidence of past physical and sexual abuse (James & Glaze, 2006). Other researchers also have noted elevated rates of experiences of interpersonal trauma, substance dependence, and associated symptoms of posttraumatic stress disorder in female offenders (Green, Miranda, Daroowalla & Siddique, 2005; Lynch, Fritch & Heath, 2012).

This multi-site study addresses critical gaps in the literature by assessing the prevalence of serious mental illness, posttraumatic stress disorder, and substance use disorders in women in jail and pathways to jail for women with and without serious mental illness.

METHODS

1. Using a randomly selected sample ($N = 491$) from rural and urban jails, this multi-site study employed the *Composite International Diagnostic Interview* (CIDI, World Health Organization, 1990), a structured diagnostic interview, to assess current and lifetime prevalence of serious mental illness (SMI, including major depression, bipolar, and psychotic spectrum disorders), posttraumatic stress disorder (PTSD), and substance use disorders (SUD) in women in jail. Women's prior access to treatment and level of functional impairment in the past 12 months was also assessed to better inform understanding of women's current treatment needs.

2. We utilized structural equation modeling to assess the associations among childhood and adult victimization, mental health, treatment services, and offending history.

3. Next, qualitative Life History Calendar interviews were conducted with a subset of the sample ($N = 115$) to explore women's pathways to jail to examine how onset of different types of criminal activity and delinquency vary as a function of mental health status and trauma exposure. Our mixed-methods research design includes quantitative event-history modeling of female inmates' life-calendar data as well as qualitative analysis of the women's life-history narratives.

4. Finally, we also interviewed corrections staff members at participating jail sites to better assess the beliefs of staff members about the prevalence of mental health difficulties in women in jail as well as staff members' perceptions about women's pathways to jail.

RESULTS

Part I: Structured diagnostic interviews ($N = 491$)

Notably, 43% of participants met criteria for a lifetime SMI and 32% met SMI criteria in the past 12 months. Substance use disorders were the most commonly occurring disorders with 82% of the sample meeting lifetime criteria for drug or alcohol abuse or dependence. Similarly, PTSD rates were high with just over half the sample (53%) meeting criteria for lifetime PTSD. Women also met criteria for multiple lifetime disorders at high rates. Finally, 30 to 45% of individuals who met criteria for a current disorder reported severely impaired functioning associated with SMI, PSTD or SUD in the past year. The majority (78-84%) of the participants who met criteria for a SMI such as Major Depressive Disorder or Bipolar had talked with a mental health professional and most indicated it was effective. In contrast, closer to half of the individuals with PTSD or substance related problems indicated that they had talked with mental health professionals about these difficulties.

Women with SMI reported greater rates of victimization and more extensive offending histories than women who did not meet criteria for lifetime SMI. In the test of our proposed model, childhood trauma and adversity significantly predicted both adult victimization experiences and mental health. However, neither childhood nor adult victimization were directly associated with offending. Instead, both forms of victimization significantly predicted mental health which in turn was the only significant predictor of offending. Mental health was also the only significant predictor of treatment. Women who reported poor mental health were 75% more likely to report using treatment services. In sum, although childhood victimization, adult trauma, and service utilization were each correlated with offending, they were not significant predictors when mental health was in the model. Instead, childhood victimization and adult trauma increased the risk of poor mental health, and poor mental health predicted a greater offending history.

Part II: Life History Calendar interviews ($N = 115$)

SMI demonstrated significant effects or trends in risk for onset of substance use, drug dealing/charges, property crime, fighting/assault, and running away. In addition, experiences of victimization predicted risk of offending. Specifically, intimate partner violence contributed to risk for commercial sex work/trading sex and drug dealing/charges. Witnessing violence contributed to risk for property offenses, fighting/assault, and using weapons. Finally, caregiver violence contributed to risk for running away.

Part III: Staff interviews ($N = 37$)

Corrections staff including supervisors, health practitioners and corrections officers/deputies indicated a general awareness that women's experiences of victimization were linked with their entry into the criminal justice system. Further, many staff were aware of women's mental health problems. In particular, they expressed concern that there were limited resources in jail for women with mental illness and that women were then released from jail with little to no assistance (e.g., housing or programs) to support their attempts to change behavior and lifestyle.

DISCUSSION

Our national sample of women in jails demonstrated high rates of mental health problems, with a majority of our participants meeting diagnostic criteria for SMI, lifetime post-traumatic stress disorder, and/or substance use disorder.

Similar to Steadman and colleagues' (2009) finding that 31% of female offenders residing in northeastern jails met criteria for a current SMI, 32% of participants in this multi-site study met criteria for a SMI in the past year. Further, the number of women meeting criteria for multiple lifetime and current disorders was high. The prevalence of SMI, PTSD, and SUD as well as rates for co-occurring disorders suggest female offenders enter (or re-enter) jail with substantial and often multiple mental health concerns, and subsequently, have complex treatment needs.

Although over half of the participants indicated prior access to treatment, a significant portion of female offenders do not appear to have treatment that is addressing their problems and helping them to improve their basic level of functioning. The levels of reported impairment combined with the frequency of SMI, PTSD, and SUD rates in this population suggest the critical need for additional resources for mental health assessment and treatment with this population.

The women with SMI reported significantly greater frequency of all forms of victimization and more extensive criminal histories. As was demonstrated in the SEM analyses, women's experiences of child and adult trauma were significant predictors of their overall mental health. The results of the SEM analyses also suggest that while child and adult victimization relate directly to women's mental health, victimization did not predict offending history directly; only mental health was directly associated with women's offending histories.

In addition to identifying this clear link between mental health problems and offending history, the data provided via the in-depth Life History Calendar interviews demonstrates how SMI is associated with increased risk of the *onset* of a number of offending behaviors and how this is exacerbated by experiences of victimization and drug use. Women with SMI were at higher risk for numerous forms of offending including running away, substance use, and drug dealing/charges. In addition to the increased risk associated with SMI, various forms of traumatic victimization predicted the onset of offending.

Understanding female offenders' pathways to offending, including both risk for onset and risk for continued offending, helps elucidate the complexity of their experiences and identify key factors and intervening variables that may ameliorate or exacerbate risk. This type of research is critical to development of gender responsive programming (Hills et al., 2004), alternatives to incarceration, and problem-solving court initiatives.

Table of Contents

Women's pathways to jail: The roles & intersections of serious mental illness & trauma

INTRODUCTION

The rate of incarceration of women has increased substantially in recent decades, with a

31% increase between 2000 and 2011 (Minton, 2012). Most recently, according the Bureau of

Justice Statistics, an estimated 11.8 million persons were admitted to local jails in 2011, with

females comprising approximately 13% of inmates (Minton, 2012). In response to the growing

number of women entering the criminal justice system, researchers have worked to identify

gender specific pathways to incarceration. One consistent finding is the high prevalence of

mental health problems in incarcerated women.

Researchers have identified elevated rates of mental illness in incarcerated populations as

compared to the general population (see Diamond, Wang, Holzer, Thomas, & Cruser, 2001).

Furthermore, female offenders report greater incidence of mental health problems and serious

mental illness than do male offenders (James & Glaze, 2006; Steadman, Osher, Robbins, Case,

& Samuels, 2009) and more frequently report experiencing multiple disorders in their lifetime

(Trestman, Ford, Zhang & Westbrock, 2007). Furthermore, in a Bureau of Justice Statistics

special report on mental health problems, James and Glaze (2006) reported that jail inmates who

reported mental health problems also indicated higher rates of substance dependence as well as

greater incidence of physical and sexual abuse in the past. Other researchers also have noted

elevated rates of experiences of interpersonal trauma, substance dependence, and associated

symptoms of posttraumatic stress in female offenders (Green, Miranda, Daroowalla & Siddique,

2005; Lynch, Fritch & Heath, 2012). Taken together, these findings suggest the potential for many

female offenders to be struggling with substantial mental health concerns including serious mental

illness (SMI), substance use disorders (SUD), and posttraumatic stress disorder (PSTD).

1

Consequently, there is increased demand for accurate needs assessments and identification of effective prevention and intervention strategies for incarcerated females.

The current study addresses critical gaps in the literature by assessing the prevalence of SMI, PTSD, and SUD in women in jail and pathways to jail for women with and without SMI. Using a randomly selected sample ($N = 491$) from rural and urban jails, this multi-site study determined current and lifetime prevalence of SMI (e.g., major depression, bipolar, and psychotic spectrum disorders), PTSD, and SUD in women in jail. Structured diagnostic interviews were utilized to assess current functioning/impairment and lifetime and current (12 month) prevalence rates. We also utilized structural equation modeling with this data to examine women's pathways to re-offending. Next, qualitative life history calendar interviews were conducted with a subset of the sample ($N = 115$) to explore women's pathways to jail. Specifically, we investigate how onset of different types of criminal activity and delinquency vary as a function of mental health status and trauma exposure. Our mixed-methods research design includes quantitative event-history modeling of female inmates' life-calendar data as well as qualitative analysis of the women's life-history narratives. Finally, we interviewed corrections staff members at participating jail sites to better assess the beliefs of staff members about the prevalence of mental health difficulties in women in jail as well as staff members' perceptions about women's pathways to jail and the resources available to assist women from re-offending and re-incarceration. The combined findings from this research project have important implications for gender-responsive, trauma-informed programming, including prevention, risk reduction, staff training, and interventions directed toward the rehabilitative needs of justice-involved women and girls.

Research on Mental Health of Female Offenders

In 2006, the Bureau of Justice Statistics released a special report entitled *Mental Health*

Problems of Prison and Jail Inmates (James & Glaze, 2006), reporting that more than half of jail inmates had mental health problems at midyear 2005. More recently, Steadman and colleagues (2009) collected data from inmates at five jails in the Northeast using structured clinical interviews. These researchers identified prevalence rates for current SMI at 31% of female offenders and 14.5% for male offenders. These authors noted that offenders' level of impairment was not assessed and encouraged future measurement of this critical aspect of mental health in subsequent studies. In a study of adults in jails in Connecticut, Trestman and colleagues (2007) assessed current and lifetime mental illness as well as functional impairment of male and female inmates. They found that 65% of males and 77% of females had a history of mental illness, with 56% of women meeting criteria for multiple lifetime disorders. Impairment was assessed with the Global Assessment of Functioning (GAF) scale, a numeric scale from 0-100 used by mental health practitioners to indicate general functioning including social, psychological and occupational functioning. Female offenders with mental illness had significantly lower GAF scores, with the average reported score suggesting moderate impairment.

Trestman and colleagues (2007) also note that it is critical to consider differences in treatment resources in jails versus prisons. Specifically, jails have similar if not higher rates of offenders entering with mental health issues (e.g., 64% of jail inmates versus 54% of state inmates, James & Glaze, 2006) but typically have fewer resources for mental health assessment, treatment, and programming given jail dependence on county level funding (Trestman et al., 2007). These high rates of mental illness are concerning for multiple reasons including likelihood of reoffending and safety risks. For example, jailed offenders with mental health problems were more likely to be dependent on drugs, to be violent recidivists, and to have served three or more prior sentences (James & Glaze, 2006). Within the jail facilities, these inmates were twice as likely to be charged with rule violations, four times as likely to be charged with assault on a correctional officer or another inmate, and three times as likely to be injured in a fight since admission. It also appears that having specific disorders may increase risk. In a survey of 16,000 male and female inmates conducted by Furthermore, Felson, Silver & Remster (2012), these authors reported that individuals with major depressive disorder and psychotic disorders were more likely than individuals with other disorders or individuals without mental illness to engage in both violent and nonviolent infractions while incarcerated. Thus, assessing for presence of specific disorders has implications both in regards to meeting treatment needs of incarcerated individuals as well as addressing the safety of corrections staff and other offenders. These findings suggest that it is critical that we work to understand the needs of jail inmates and how addressing these needs (or not) impacts jail operations to best inform funding decisions as well as providing information that would facilitate corrections-community partnerships to address these needs.

Research on Trauma & Adversity among Female Offenders

Numerous studies have indicated high rates of trauma exposure among incarcerated women and girls (Belknap & Holsinger, 2006; Browne, Miller, & Maguin, 1999; Carlson & Shafer, 2010; DeHart, 2008; Green et al., 2005; Lynch et. al., 2012). Green and colleagues (2005) interviewed 100 female jail inmates regarding trauma exposure and mental health functioning. An overwhelming majority (98%) of these women reported traumatic exposure, most commonly partner violence (71%) or childhood trauma (62%). Lynch, Fritch, and Health (2012) found that 90% of a sample of incarcerated women ($N = 102$) reported physical and sexual violence from their partners in the year prior to incarceration, and that many women described polyvictimization throughout their lifetime, including chronic and severe abuse. DeHart (DeHart, 2009; DeHart & Moran, in press) interviewed justice-involved girls in group homes or long-term commitment and found that a majority had been victimized multiple times as well as experienced multiple adverse childhood events (ACEs; Felitti & Anda, 2009) such as death of a family member, caregiver imprisonment or addiction, or persistent family conflict.

Recognizing the extent and dynamics of incarcerated women's trauma exposure is critical for multiple reasons. Foremost, individuals with multiple experiences of trauma are at greater risk of developing psychological problems (Hedtke, Ruggiero, Fitzgerald, Zinzow, Saunders, Resnick, et al., 2008; Turner, Finklehor & Ormrod, 2005). For example, mental health problems such as PTSD, depression and substance disorders are not only associated with lifetime experience of violence, but the odds of experiencing these mental health difficulties increase with the accumulation of experiences of different types of interpersonal violence (Hedtke et al., 2008). In a study with 1441 female inmates, Carlson and Shafer (2010) noted that 30% indicated they had been diagnosed with a mental disorder and that this was strongly associated with prior traumatic childhood events. Similarly, Lynch, Fritch, & Health (2012) found the number of different types of interpersonal violence experienced by incarcerated women significantly predicted current symptoms of depression, PTSD, and substance dependence.

Further, experiences of interpersonal violence are clearly linked to entry into the criminal justice system. For example, women who were abused or neglected as children are twice as likely to be arrested as adults than nonabused women (Widom, 2000). Grella, Stein, and Greenwell (2005) utilized structural equation modeling to examine the associations among varied abuse experiences, adolescent conduct problems, substance use, and adult criminal behaviors for 440 adult women on parole. Grella and her colleagues (2005) found that females who experienced interpersonal violence as children were more likely to engage in problematic behaviors as youths and subsequently to commit crimes as adults. DeHart (2008) reported similar findings from qualitative interviews with

60 women in prison. The majority of these women had experienced multiple traumas, and many explicitly connected traumatic experiences (e.g., childhood sexual abuse) with the onset of criminal behaviors (e.g., running away, using illicit drugs). DeHart noted that the unrelenting nature of multiple traumas in conjunction with additional adverse childhood events (e.g., caregiver use of drugs, abandonment, exploitation) normalizes behaviors like trading sex for shelter or drugs during adolescence or women retaliating violently against abusive partners. In a survey of 163 girls, Belknap and Holsinger (2008) noted that more than half the girls indicated direct links between their abuse experiences and their subsequent offending. These studies emphasize the necessity of understanding adolescent and adult pathways to identify risks for offending as well as potential points for prevention and intervention. In the current study, we assess the prevalence of mental illness and explore pathways to jail for women with and without mental illness in four regions of the U.S. A final goal was to understand the extent to which corrections staff were aware of the prevalence of mental health difficulties in female offenders as well as learning about their perceptions about female offenders' needs and pathways to incarceration.

For increased clarity, methods and results for each of the three parts of the study are described below. First, we review methods and results for the structured diagnostic interviews (Part I), then the life history calendar interviews (Part II), and finally for the staff interviews (Part III).

METHODS AND RESULTS

The project methodology was approved by human subjects review boards at each sampling site.

PART I: The Structured Diagnostic Interviews

Methods

Participants

Sampling was conducted in four geographically distinct regions of the U.S.—the

Southwest, Mid-Atlantic, Northwest, and Deep South, with investigators located in Colorado, District of Columbia, Idaho, and South Carolina. Within each region, up to three counties were selected for sampling, with selected counties representing a variation across urban/rural classifications, crime and victimization trends, and inmate demographics.

A total of 491 women in jail, either pre- (51%) or post-conviction (49%), participated in structured diagnostic interviews. Interviews were conducted at a total of nine jails across the four regions. Facilities ranged in size, housing anywhere from 30 to 335 women. Approximately 43 % of the participants were housed in six jails, four that were located in rural areas with fewer than 500 people per square mile, and two in nonmetro areas (e.g., areas with population centers under 50,000, U.S. Census Bureau, 2010, see Table 1).

Table 1

Jail Demographic Information

U.S. Region	State	County	Average daily jail female census	Rural-Urban code	Persons per square mile	Sample (*N*=491)
Southwest	Colorado	Denver	335	Metro	3922.6	204
Mid-Atlantic	Virginia	Arlington	50	Metro	7993.6	29
	Maryland	Prince George's	82	Metro	134.7	64
Northwest	Idaho	Bannock	72	Metro	74.5	29
		Bonneville	86	Metro	55.9	58
		Caribou	30	Non-metro	3.9	23
Deep South	South Carolina	Lexington	67	Metro	375.4	21
		Orange	34	Non-metro	83.6	16
		Richland	142	Metro	507.9	47

The women ranged in age from 17 to 62 with an average age of 35 ($SD = 10.65$) and a median age of 33. Just over half (56%) had children under the age of 18. Prior to their incarceration, 33% were employed full time, 11% part-time, and 6.7 % indicated they received SSI/disability support. Approximately a third had completed high school, 26% reported some high school, and 36% reported attending at least some college. Women identified as white/Caucasian (38%), African American/Black (37%), Latina (15%), American Indian (4%), Asian/Pacific Islander (1%), multiethnic (2%) and other ethnic identities (3%). Approximately a quarter (25%) were first time offenders and 16% were charged with or convicted of a violent crime. Charges are listed below in Table 2.

Table 2

Charges Leading to Incarceration

Type of offense	Percent of sample ($N = 491$)
Probation/PV	21
Drug possession	14
Other	12
Assault/battery/DV	11
Larceny/theft	11
Fraud/forgery	8
DUI	7
Other vehicle offense	5
Prostitution	4
Murder/manslaughter	2
Burglary/home invasion	2
Child abuse	1
Weapons	1
Sexual offense	0.4

Measures

Female offender demographics of age, education, income prior to incarceration, race/ethnicity, relationship status, parent status, charges, and length of sentence were collected as part of the structured interview.

The *Composite International Diagnostic Interview* (CIDI) is a widely used structured interview developed by the World Health Organization (1990). The CIDI can be used to assess lifetime and 12 month disorders according to criteria of the ICD-10 and DSM-IV. Items in the CIDI also access level of impairment for each disorder, treatment access, and symptom severity. The CIDI is designed for use by trained non-clinician interviewers. Several national prevalence studies have utilized the CIDI, allowing comparisons of prevalence rates between incarcerated and non-incarcerated populations. The CIDI paper and pencil (PAPI v7) structured interview modules for major depression, bipolar, PTSD, and substance dependence and abuse disorders were utilized in this study. The CIDI screening items for depression, bipolar, and psychotic spectrum disorders were administered to all participants and corresponding modules were administered to participants who screened positively. The PTSD, illegal substance, and alcohol use modules were administered to all participants.

The CIDI contains an extensive screening section for the psychotic disorders but does not assess all relevant criteria. Participants who screened positively on the CIDI psychotic screening items were also administered an adapted version of the SCID psychotic module to assess whether an individual met criteria for Schizophrenia, Schizophreniform, Schizoaffective, Delusional Disorder and Brief Psychotic Disorder. See Appendix A for further discussion of this adaptation. Finally, the CIDI includes items assessing whether an individual has seen a professional for mental health treatment and inquires whether this was effective. In consideration of recommendations in the literature that treatment quality be assessed in greater depth, we also included several of the recommended quality of care items from the 2004 Mental Health report published by the Substance Abuse and Mental Health Services Administration (SAMHSA, see Appendix B).

Next, given our focus on traumatic experiences and pathways of female offenders, we expanded the assessment of trauma exposure in the CIDI from presence/absence of the event to a five point frequency scale (from once to more than 4 times) and we also adapted items from the Life Stressor Checklist- Revised (Wolfe & Kimerling, 1997) and the Turner Adversity Scale (Turner et al., 2006). For example, we modified items to assess childhood (before age 16) versus adult experiences of abuse as well as including items to assess nonvictimization adversity such as caregiver addiction and incarceration. Finally, the full interview was transcribed into Spanish by an ATA-certified translator for administration to Spanish-speaking participants.

Procedures

Inmate names and charges were obtained from participating facilities. Offenders were randomly selected, called out, and invited to participate in a study of women's pathways to jail, mental health and life experiences by a trained interviewer. Inmates who were unavailable at the time their name was selected were invited on the subsequent interview date. Once informed consent was obtained, interviews were conducted in private, enclosed rooms. Participants had the option to interview in English or Spanish. Compensation for the interview varied by jail and included a snack, ten dollars deposited in the individual's canteen account, or funds applied towards the purchase of materials for inmates use at the jail (e.g., self-help books). The structured diagnostic interviews lasted from one hour to six hours with an average of two hours per interview ($M = 1.95$, $SD = .91$).

We obtained de-identified data on age, ethnicity, and charges for offenders who declined to participate in the study from each jail in order to assess whether there were differences between individuals who participated and those who did not. Participants who declined to participate ($N = 142$) did not differ by age or by offense type (violent/non-violent). Participants who declined differed significantly by ethnicity. Individuals who identified as African American (79%

accepted) and Latina (85% accepted) participated at similar rates to Caucasians (75% accepted) and at significantly higher rates than the small number of randomly selected American Indians ($N = 15$, 47% declined, see Table 3).

Table 3

Percentage of Individuals Accepting or Declining to Interview by Ethnicity

Participant ethnic identity	Accept %	Decline %
Caucasian ($n = 279$)	74.6	25.4
African American ($n = 242$)	78.9	21.1
Latina ($n = 79$)	84.8	15.2
American Indian ($n = 15$)	53.3	46.7
Other ($n = 17$)	94	6

Participation also varied in response to the form of compensation offered. Individuals in the two jails (one in Idaho and one in South Carolina) where compensation was limited to a donation to a general fund declined at significantly higher rates (50%) than individuals who received $10 deposited into their canteen (0-21%) or snacks (21%). However, it is important to note that compensation was not confounded with region as there were multiple facilities with varied forms of compensation in these two regions.

A total of 15 women were excluded from the structured diagnostic interviews: five were excluded due to threat of violence and five due to acute distress at the time of the invitation to interview. Finally, five were excluded due to IRB restrictions in one of the four regions prohibiting interviews with pre-sentence offenders charged with homicide, first degree assault or felony sex charges. Although this restriction was in place, it is important to note that overall participation by individuals who committed violent crimes was not lower in this region.

Analyses

All statistical analyses were carried out using IBM SPSS software version 20.00 (IBM Software,

Somers, NY).

Descriptive statistics.

Descriptive statistics were computed to ascertain lifetime prevalence of mental disorders, substance use, offending, victimization, and childhood non-victimization adversity.

Structural equation modeling.

Structural equation modeling (SEM) was utilized to test the proposed model using Mplus (see Figure 1). SEM is a statistical technique that simultaneously estimates complex relationships among multiple variables. Model fit was evaluated by the χ^2 goodness-of-fit statistic and three fit indices - Comparative Fit Index (CFI; Bentler, 1990), Tucker Lewis Index (TLI; Tucker & Lewis, 1973), and root mean square of approximation (RMSEA; Steiger & Lind, 1980). The χ^2 goodness-of-fit statistic evaluates the difference between the data and the fitted covariance matrices, i.e., the hypothetical model (Bentler & Bonnet, 1980). An insignificant value indicates a good fit. However, the χ^2 test becomes overly conservative when sample size increases (Bentler, 1990). Our sample is large ($N = 491$), making it more likely to obtain a significant χ^2 value. An alternative is to use χ^2/df (degrees of freedom of the model). If the ratio is not bigger than 2, we consider the hypothesized model to fit the data well (Schumaker & Lomax, 2010).

Additionally, other indices are also used to evaluate model fit. A value of .9 or above on fit indices such as the CFI and TLI indicates a good fit, while a value of .95 and above indicates an excellent fit (Hu & Bentler, 1999). Values of .06 or below on the root mean square of approximation (RMSEA) indicate a good fit (Hu & Bentler, 1999). Mediation analyses were performed using the product-of-coefficients approach (MacKinnon et al., 2002; MacKinnon, 2008). Specifically two methods were used, the Sobel Z test (Sobel, 1982), and MacKinnon's asymmetric confidence interval (MacKinnon et al., 2007; MacKinnon, 2008). Sobel *Z* test is

highly conservative, therefore we supplemented it with asymmetric confidence interval, a

statistically more powerful test (MacKinnon et al., 2002). If the 95% asymmetric confidence

interval does not include zero, the mediation effect is statistically significant.

Figure 1: Proposed model

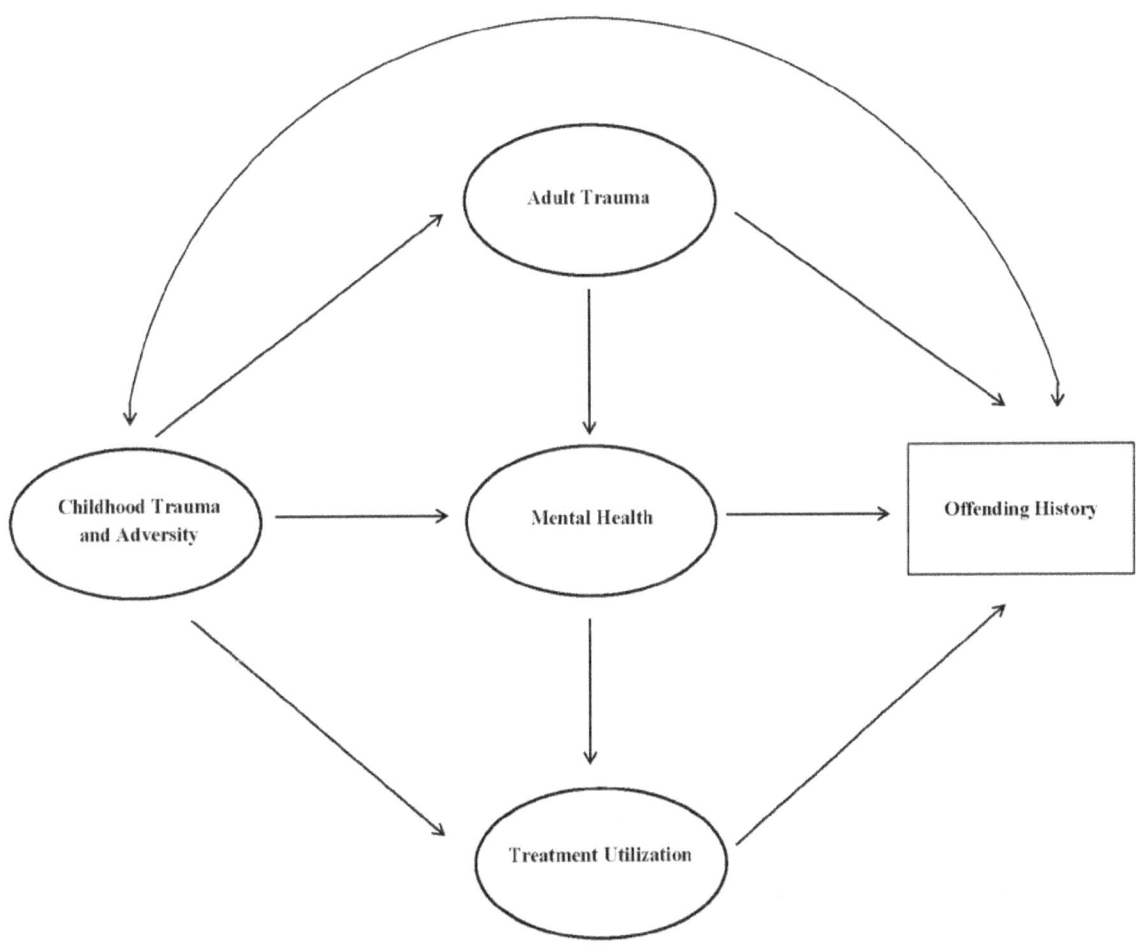

Results

Findings are reported below for the prevalence of the assessed disorders, co-occurring

disorders, and regional differences in prevalence rates. The women's current level of functioning and access to treatment is also presented. Finally, we describe substance use, extent of trauma exposure/victimization, and the associations among mental health, victimization, and offending.

Prevalence of mental disorders

A major focus of our study was to assess the prevalence of SMI and co-occurring PTSD and SUD. Table 4 illustrates that the vast majority of women in our sample met diagnostic criteria for at least one of the disorders assessed. Only 9% did not meet criteria for a lifetime diagnosis of SMI, PTSD, or SUD and only 30% of participants did not meet criteria for a SMI, PTSD, or a SUD in the past 12 months. Notably, 43% of participants met criteria for a lifetime SMI and 32% met SMI criteria in the past 12 months. Major depression was the most common lifetime and 12 month SMI, followed by Bipolar disorder. Comparatively few participants (4%) met criteria for disorders in the Schizophrenia spectrum. Substance use disorders were the most commonly occurring disorders with 82% of the sample meeting lifetime criteria for drug or alcohol abuse or dependence. Similarly, PTSD rates were high with just over half the sample (53%) meeting criteria for lifetime PTSD.

These women also met criteria for multiple disorders. Approximately one in five (22%) met criteria for two disorders in the past 12 months and one in four (24%) reported experiencing three disorders in their lifetime. Specifically, 29% met criteria for lifetime SMI and PTSD, 33% met criteria for lifetime SMI and SUD, and about one in five, 23%, met criteria for SMI, PTSD, and SUD in their lifetime. In the past 12 months, 20% of participants met criteria for SUD and SMI, 14% of participants met criteria for both PTSD and SMI, and 9% met criteria for SMI, PTSD, and SUD. Finally, 46% of the sample met criteria for lifetime PTSD and SUD while 18% met criteria for both in the past 12 months.

Table 4

Prevalence of Lifetime and Current (12 Month) Mental Disorders

Type of disorder	Percent of sample (N = 491)	
	Lifetime %	Current (12 Month) %
Serious mental illness	**43**	**32**
Major Depression	28	22
Bipolar	15	8
Schizophrenia spectrum	4	4
Brief Psychotic disorder	14	8
Posttraumatic stress disorder	**53**	**28**
Substance use disorder	**82**	**53**
Alcohol Abuse	25	9
Alcohol Dependence	39	17
Drug Abuse	12	6
Drug Dependence	56	33

There were no significant differences in rates of SMI, PTSD or SUD in participants in county jails in rural versus urban locations. In contrast, there were significant regional differences with participants in the Maryland/Virginia area meeting criteria for lifetime SMI significantly less than the Idaho and Colorado participants ($\chi^2(3)$=17.133, $p < .001$). Idaho participants also met criteria for lifetime PTSD significantly more often than participants in any other region ($\chi^2(3)$=24.824, , $p < .000$) and met criteria for lifetime SUD significantly more often than participants in the Maryland/Virginia area (See Figure 2).

While we cannot determine with certainty the reason for regional differences, it appears the results of this project are similar to those from a recent national study of SMI. A 2011 report, *The NSDUH Report: State Estimates of Adult Mental Illness*, from SAMHSA noted differences in SMI by state and reported 12 month SMI at 5.8% in Idaho, 5.2% Colorado, 4.1% in South Carolina, 3.9% in Maryland and 3.6% in Virginia. In particular, this report notes that Idaho residents reported SMI rates among the highest in the country while residents of Maryland and

Virginia were among those reporting the lowest rates nationwide.

Figure 2. Regional differences in the prevalence of lifetime mental health disorders

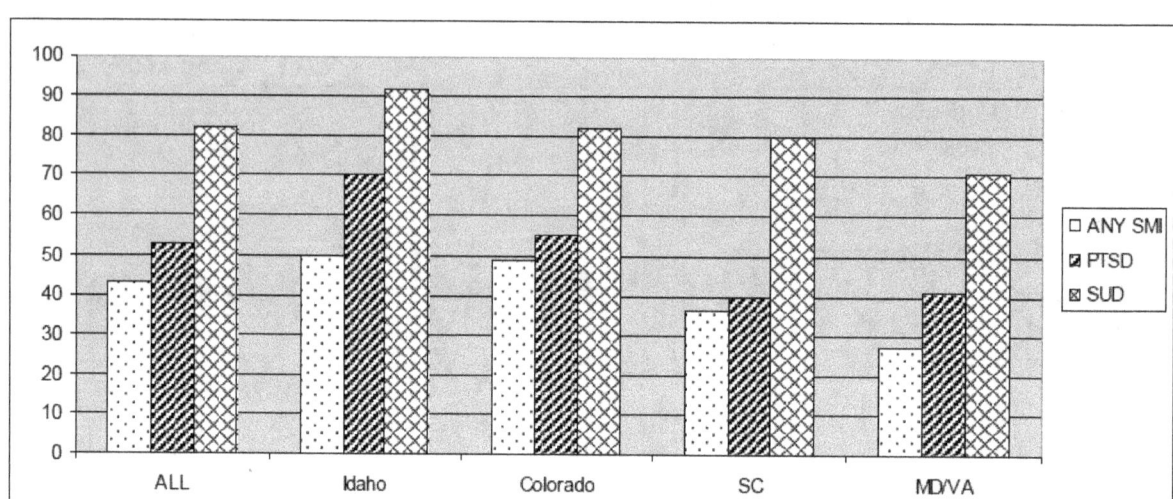

Impairment associated with SMI, PTSD and SUD

When participants endorsed problems in the past year in a particular module (e.g.,

depression), they were then asked to indicate their worst functioning in the past twelve months

on a scale of 0 to 10, where a "0" indicated no interference, 1-3 indicates mild interference, 4-6

moderate interference, 7-9 severe interference, and a "10" indicated very severe interference.

Participants indicated their functioning level for their home management (e.g., grocery shopping,

cleaning), ability to work, ability to form and maintain close relationships, and social life. Of

those who indicated impairment because of SMI in the past 12 months, 45% endorse an average

impairment across the four areas of a "7" or higher, suggesting severe to very severe levels of

impairment. Similarly, for individuals who met criteria for PTSD in the past 12 months, 42%

reported an average of "7" or greater impairment in function while 30% of those who met SUD

criteria in the past 12 months indicated severe to very severe problems in functioning. On

average, participants reported impairment from SMI, PTSD, and SUD in the moderate interference range (see Table 5).

Table 5

Average 12 Month Overall Impairment for Individuals with SMI, PTSD and SUD

Impairment	*N*	*M*	*SD*
SMI Impairment	152	6.21	2.81
PTSD Impairment	130	6.17	2.65
SUD Impairment	263	4.94	3.37

Treatment Access and Quality prior to incarceration

Participants also reported their access to mental health professionals, the effectiveness of their interactions with professionals, and also whether they had been hospitalized, prescribed medications, and for SUD, self-help group utilization (see Tables 6 and 7). The majority of the participants who met criteria for SMI had talked with a mental health professional and most indicated it was effective. In contrast, closer to half of the individuals with PTSD or substance related problems indicated that they had talked with mental health professionals about these difficulties.

Table 6

Lifetime Mental Health Treatment Access Prior to Incarceration

Mental health problems	Talk to a professional	Effective treatment	Hospitalized	Medication
Depression	84% 159 of 189	64% 101 of 159	40% 76 of 189	83% 155 of 187
Bipolar	78% 105 of 135	71% 75 of 101	30% 41 of 135	72% 95 of 132
Psychotic Spectrum	59% 92 of 155		25% 39 of 159	68% 102 of 149
PTSD	51% 190 of 369	62% 119 of 190	13% 64 of 368	45% 160 of 354

Table 7

Lifetime Treatment Access for Substance Use Prior to Incarceration

Substance problems	Talk to a professional	Effective treatment	Hospitalized	Medication	Self-Help/ 12 Step
Illegal Substances	51% 199 of 388	72.5% 145 of 200	19% 76 of 395	13% 51 of 382	60.5% 233 of 388
Alcohol	36.5% 138 of 378	69% 96 of 138	20% 76 of 375	12% 45 of 365	58% 217 of 375

Participants also rated the quality and outcome effectiveness of their most recent treatment experience prior to incarceration. Quality was measured with a five point scale from strongly disagree (1) to strongly agree (5) with five items assessing the ability to see the practitioner quickly, the amount of time the practitioner spent with the individual, access to information about different services, sufficient information about how to handle the condition, and cultural sensitivity of the service provider. Approximately half of the sample (55%) reported on the quality of their most recent treatment experience prior to incarceration. Among these individuals, 20% disagreed or disagreed strongly that they had received quality mental health treatment and one in three (36%) disagreed or disagreed strongly that their symptoms and functioning improved. About 10% of participants rated substance focused treatment quality as poor and one in four (26%) disagreed that their symptoms and functioning improved. Thus, it appears that a notable minority of individuals seeking treatment do not appear to be benefiting from that treatment.

Substance use

Given the majority of the participants met criteria for a SUD disorder in their lifetime and that one in three met criteria for both lifetime SMI and SUD, it is important to discuss briefly what substances women indicated they used. As illustrated in Table 8, only 10% of the sample indicated no drug abuse ever. Approximately 25% reported abuse of six or more substances with an average of 3.8 and median of three drugs abused. Marijuana and cocaine appear to be the most commonly used substances. The majority of women (90%) also reported drinking alcohol at some point, with about one third reporting drinking by age 15, 60% by age 18, and 20% reporting they drank every day or nearly every day in the 12 months prior to incarceration.

Table 8

Prevalence of Self-Reported Drug Abuse

Type of substance	Percent of sample ($N = 491$)
No substance use	10
Marijuana	84
Cocaine	65
Pain killers	36
Stimulants (e.g., methamphetamine)	34
Sedatives	29
Other drug use	8

Victimization

Participants indicated exposure to traumatic events as part of assessment of life threatening events in the PTSD module. As noted in the methods section, we further assessed for specific forms of victimization (e.g., childhood versus adulthood) and adversity for the purpose of better understanding the range of women's experiences as well as examining how these experiences contribute to paths to offending. The women's reported rates of victimization are depicted in Figure 3.

Figure 3. Victimization and adversity Rates (*N* = 491)

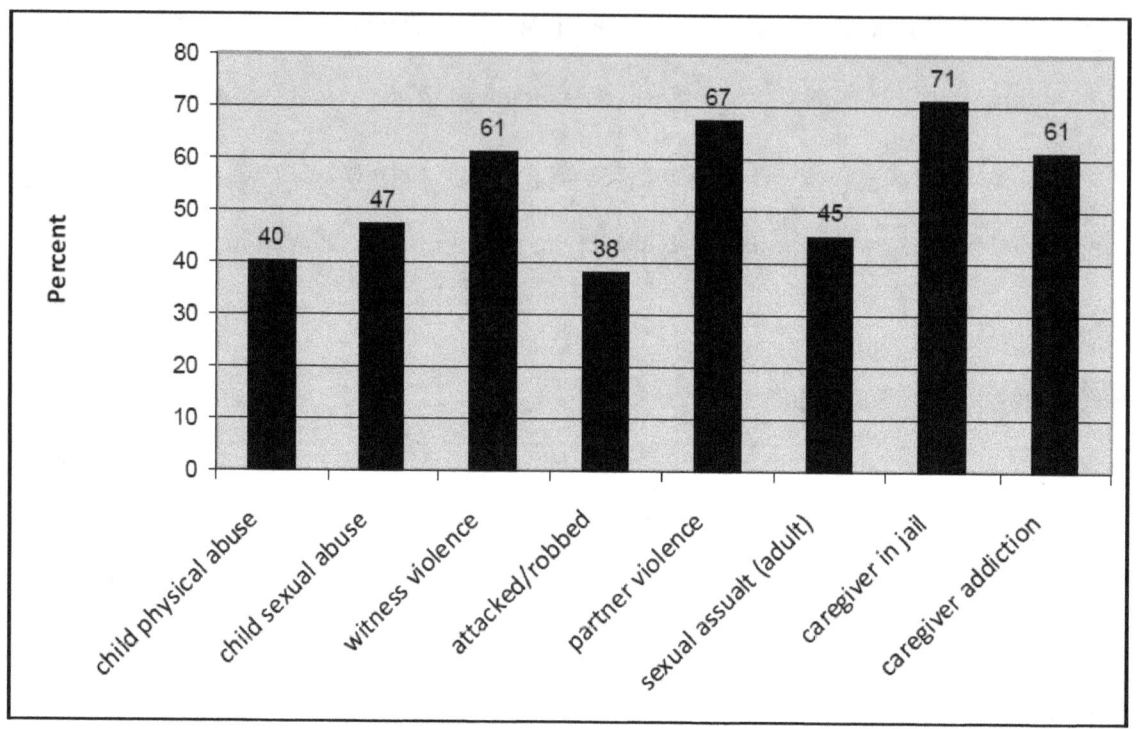

It is further important to note that those participants who met criteria for lifetime SMI reported

significantly higher rates of each form of victimization (see Table 9).

Table 9

Rates of Victimization and Adversity for Women With and Without Lifetime SMI

Type of trauma	*N*	Mean	*SD*	*SE*	*F*
Child physical abuse	491	1.71	2.25	.10	24.87*
No SMI	280	1.28	2.07	.12	
SMI	211	2.28	2.36	.16	
Child Sexual Abuse	485	2.35	3.43	.16	22.01*
No SMI	276	1.74	3.02	.18	
SMI	209	2.54	3.75	.26	
Caregiver in jail/prison	485	2.30	2.04	.09	13.58*
No SMI	276	2.00	1.96	.12	
SMI	209	2.68	2.08	.14	
Caregiver addiction	489	2.64	2.36	.11	16.43*
No SMI	280	2.27	2.33	.14	
SMI	209	3.12	2.31	.16	
Witnessed violence	489	3.13	3.28	.15	22.64*
No SMI	279	2.64	3.12	.19	
SMI	210	3.78	3.39	.23	
Adult attacked	490	.91	1.50	.07	14.92*
No SMI	280	.69	1.35	.08	
SMI	210	1.2	1.65	.11	
Adult partner violence	491	2.11	2.20	.10	15.71*
No SMI	280	2.18	2.17	.13	
SMI	211	2.97	2.17	.15	
Adult sexual violence	490	2.11	3.24	.15	22.64*
No SMI	280	1.52	2.75	.16	
SMI	210	2.90	3.65	.25	

Note. *$p < .001$

SMI, Offending History and Violent Crimes

The average number of convictions for participants in this sample was 3.78 (*SD* = 7.36) with a median of two former convictions and one in four women reporting four or more convictions at the time of the current incarceration. Women with SMI reported a greater number of prior convictions (*M = 4.80, SD = 9.08*) than did women without SMI (*M = 3.01, SD =5.63*), $t(461)$= -2.61, $p < .01$.

As noted above, approximately 16% of the sample were charged with or convicted of a violent crime. Individuals with SMI were more likely to be charged with or have committed a violent crime than women without SMI, $\chi^2(1) = 3.95$, $p< .05$.

Victimization, Mental Health, and Treatment as Predictors of Offending

As stated in previous sections, we hypothesized that childhood victimization and adversity, adult victimization, mental health, and utilization of treatment would be associated with offending history (i.e., the number of crimes committed) in our participants. More specifically, we hypothesized that childhood victimization predicted adult victimization, current mental health, and utilization of service and these three factors in turn predicted offending. Structural equation modeling (SEM) was used to test these hypotheses.

Measurement model.

First, we tested how well our indicators represented the four latent constructs in the proposed model: childhood victimization and adversity, adult victimization, mental health, and treatment utilization and quality (See Figure 4). All indicators loaded significantly ($p < .001$) on the latent constructs they measured, suggesting the instruments were good measures of the four latent constructs. Specifically, child victimization and adversity was represented by indicators for the frequency of physical abuse, witnessing violence, sexual abuse, corruption (e.g., a parent

22

asked the offender as a child to use or sell drugs), and caregiver addiction during childhood.

Loadings were strong, ranging from .51 to .65. Adult victimization consisted of frequency of

partner violence, sexual assaults, witnessing violence, and non-intimate physical attacks. Again,

loadings were strong (.46 to .73).

Figure 4: Measurement model

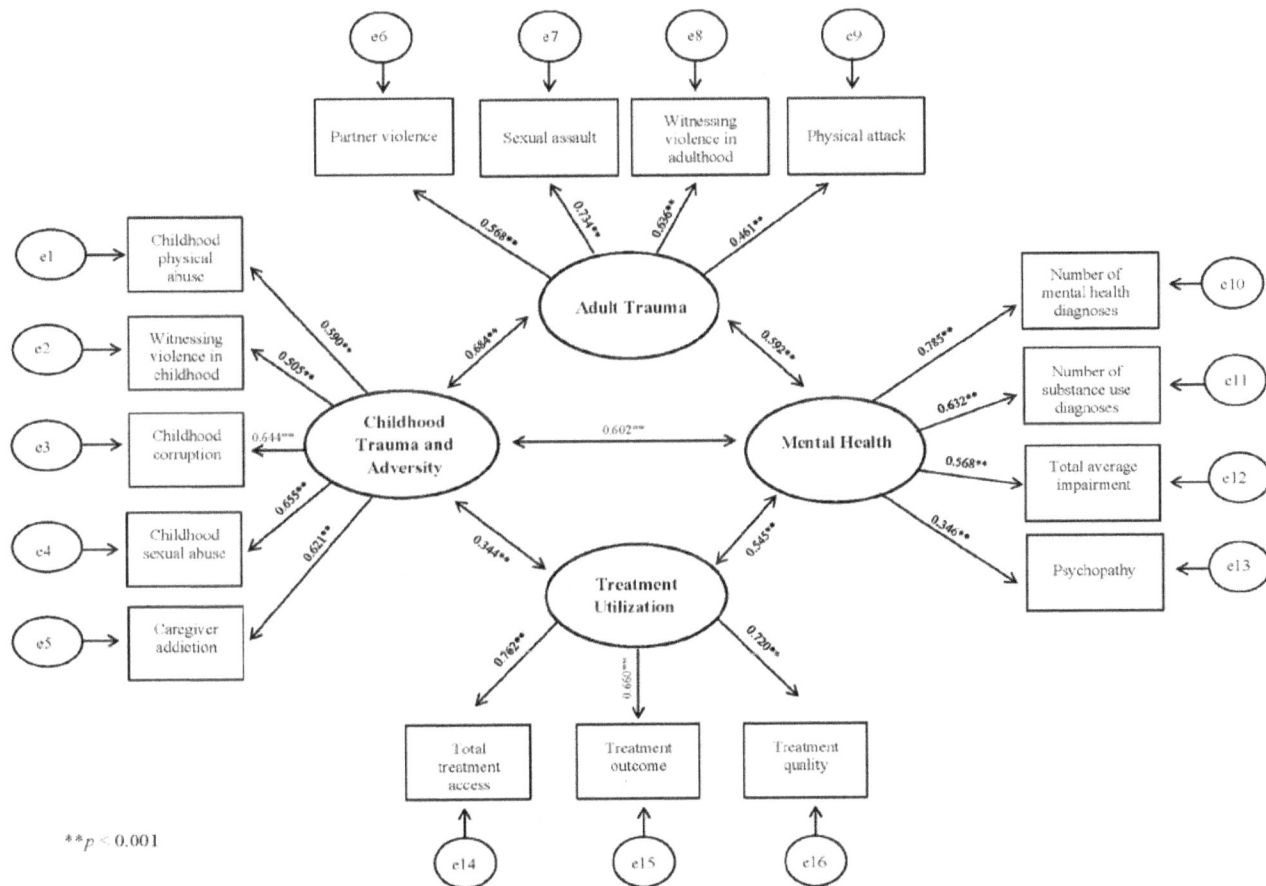

The latent variable representing mental health included indicators of the number of

lifetime mental health diagnoses, number of lifetime substance use disorders, average level of

current impairment, and the psychopathy score. Loadings ranged from .73 for number of mental

health diagnoses to .35 for the psychopathy score. Although the psychopathy loading is not as

strong, and in fact, psychopathy was negatively correlated with the number of mental health diagnoses ($r = -.224$, $p <.009$), the model demonstrated a better fit when this indicator was included.

Treatment utilization and quality was represented by indicators for the total number of treatments accessed, average outcome for the most recent treatment, and average quality of the most recent treatment. Loadings ranged from .66 to .72. As expected, all of the latent variables correlated significantly with one another (see Figure 4). Finally, the fit statistics also demonstrate that the measurement model fit the data well, (χ^2 /df = 1.50, CFI = .96, TLI = .95, RMSEA = .03).

Structural model.

Next, we tested the structural model, examining the relationships among the four constructs and the observed outcome variable representing criminal offending history. The results are presented in Figure 5. Childhood victimization significantly predicted adult trauma ($\beta = .68$ (.06), $p < .001$). Women who had a history of childhood trauma and adversity were significantly more likely to report being traumatized as an adult. Adult trauma in turn predicted poorer mental health ($\beta = .38$ (.10), $p<.001$). Mediation analyses using the product-of-coefficient approach (MacKinnon et al., 2002; MacKinnon, 2008) demonstrated that adult trauma significantly mediated the effect of childhood victimization on mental health (Sobel $Z = 3.50$, $p< .001$; 95% asymmetric confidence interval = .12 - .41). Controlling for adult trauma, childhood victimization also had a direct effect on current mental health ($\beta = .31$ (.11), $p < .005$). This indicated that regardless of whether one experienced adult trauma, having been victimized in childhood alone increased the risk of poorer mental health.

Mental health predicted treatment service utilization ($\beta = .56$ (.05), Odds ratio=1.75, $p<.001$). Women who reported poorer mental health were 75% more likely to report using

24

treatment services. However, treatment utilization was not significantly associated with offending history. In addition, neither childhood victimization and adversity nor adult victimization directly predicted offending history. Instead, mental health mediated the relationships between both forms of victimization and offending. Mental health mediated the effect of childhood victimization on offending history (Sobel $Z = 2.51$, $p < .05$; 95% asymmetric confidence interval = .04 -.24) and the effect of adult victimization on offending (Sobel $Z = 3.07$, $p < .001$; 95% asymmetric confidence interval = .07-.26).

Figure 5. A test of a model of victimization, mental health, and treatment as predictors of offending.

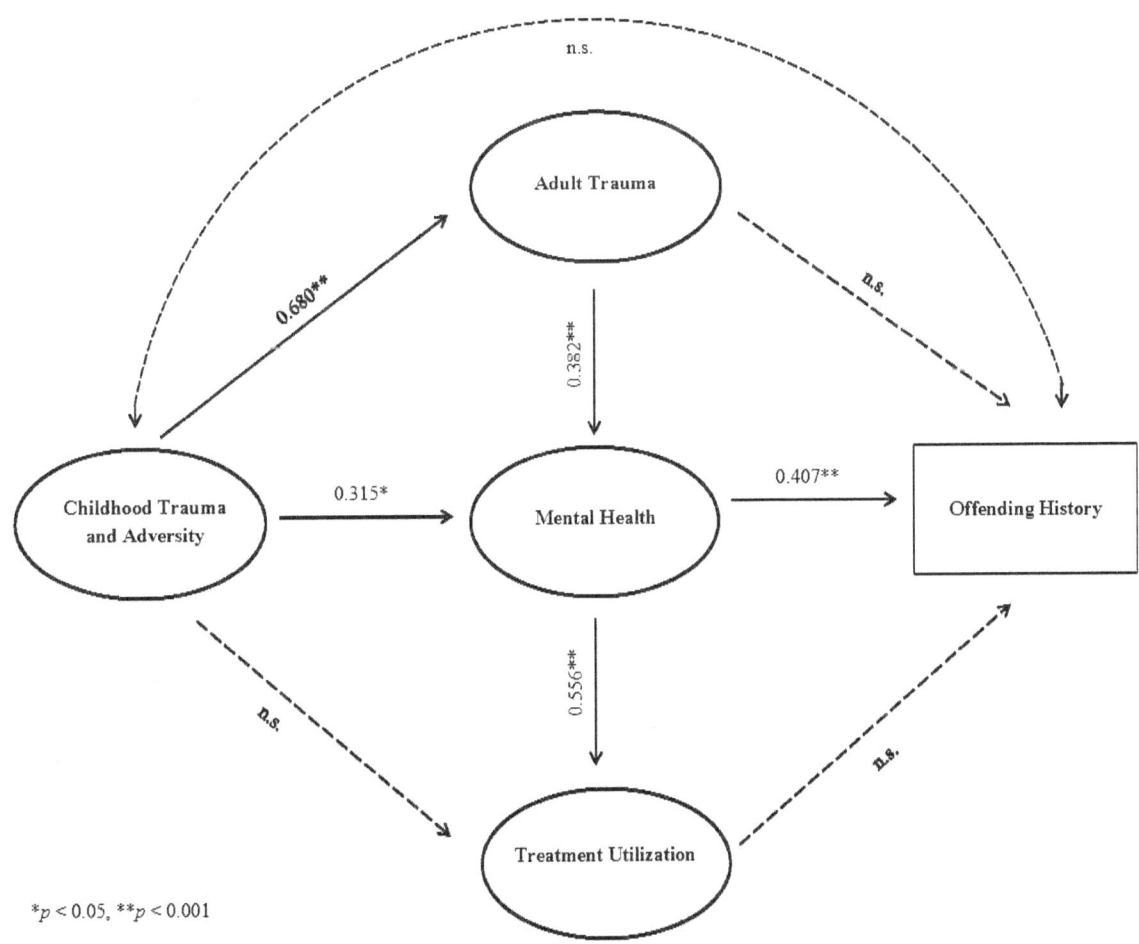

In sum, mental health was the only significant direct predictor of offending history (e.g., the number of crime committed) among the participants. Although childhood victimization, adult trauma, and service utilization were each correlated with offending, they were not significant predictors when mental health was in the model. Instead, childhood victimization and adult trauma increased the risk of poor mental health, and poor mental health increased the number of crimes committed. Although mental health was associated with treatment utilization, treatment utilization did not predict offending when mental health was controlled for in the model. The overall fit indices of the structural model indicate that our hypothesized model fits the data well ($\chi^2 = (101)$ 133.42, p 05, $\chi^2/df = 1.32$, CFI= .96, TLI = .95, RMSEA = .03).

It is important to note that we could not test for group differences between individuals with and without SMI given the clear overlap between SMI and the mental health construct in the model because of linear dependency issues. Instead, we can conclude that individuals with more complex mental health presentations (greater numbers of lifetime mental health and substance use disorders and greater impairment) have more extensive criminal offending histories.

Part II: The Life History Calendar Interviews

Methods

Participants

About one quarter of the overall sample ($N = 115$) participated in a second interview, the qualitative Life History Calendar interview, across the four project sites (CO n = 30, ID n = 30, SC n = 30, and VA/MD n = 25). Women ranged in age from 17 to 55, with the mean and median age of 34 years. Women identified as White (41%), African American/Black (40%), Hispanic/Latina (10%), Native American (4%), and multiracial (4%). Of these women, 27% did not complete high school, 27% completed high school or earned a GED, and 46% completed at least some college. Nearly half of women were employed prior to their incarceration, and the median income was approximately $15,000 in the prior twelve months for women in our sample. These figures are roughly concordant with demographics of the overall study sample. However, it is important to note that due to the detailed nature of the life history interview, state variations in reporting mandates, and differences in mandated reporter status among interviewers, primarily post-conviction women were invited to participate in life history calendar interviews, although both pre- and post-conviction women were interviewed at one site[1].

Measures

The Life History Calendar (LHC) is an established tool to optimize accuracy in event timing/sequencing data (Axinn et al. 1999; Belli, 1998; Freedman et al., 1988). The LHC tool is a calendar-like matrix, providing visual cues that enhances both interviewee and interviewer performance in mapping event history information. To facilitate lifetime recall, column headings were organized in terms of major life stages (e.g., infancy/early childhood, mid/late childhood, early adolescence, mid/late adolescence, twenties, thirties, forties, fifties, and late adulthood). Row headings denoted categories of life events including schools, households/neighborhoods, work, childhood family problems, relationship partners, pregnancy/children, alcohol/drug use, crime/delinquency, victimization, mental health, and supports. With the respondent's assistance, the LHC interviewer maps memorable life experiences on the LHC (e.g., jobs, living arrangements). These salient cues then provide a temporal context for recall of events that may be less salient in time (e.g., "The abuse happened when I was in third grade and lived with my aunt"). The LHC's rows and columns encourage recall at both thematic and temporal levels, and thereby increases power of autobiographical memory (Axinn et al. 1999; Belli, 1998, see

---

[1] Exploratory analyses indicate that this site was similar to other sites in frequency of key variables.

Appendix C). Field notes were used to supplement the life history calendar to document data obtained from these qualitative interviews.

Criminologists have used the LHC method with populations including incarcerated offenders, with calendar time frames ranging from a single month to a forty-year period; findings indicate strong test-retest reliability and validity, as well as responsiveness to administration needs of those with unstable lives and cognitive difficulties (Sutton, 2010; Sutton et al., 2011). Here, as in that research, the LHC was used *in conjunction* with *lifetime* victimization measures. That is, we administered items verbatim from the victimization measure, with each item denoted as a calendar row.

The measure of exposure to violence was the Juvenile Victimization Questionnaire, one of the most rigorously constructed measures of exposure to violence (Hamby & Finkelhor, 2004). The JVQ includes items on child maltreatment, gang violence, dating violence, sexual victimization, and witnessing/indirect victimization. For our interviews of adult women, we adapted the self-report version of the JVQ for lifetime retrospective administration (Finkelhor, Ormrod, Turner, & Hamby, 2005). Women were asked the first time they remembered each event happening and about subsequent times if it happened more than once. Follow-up prompts addressed number of times the victimization occurred, relationship to perpetrator, whether physical injury occurred, and questions specific to the victimization.

Adverse childhood events were measured using Turner et al.'s (2006) items on non-victimization adversity, including family illnesses and deaths, caregiver unemployment or imprisonment, family addictions or mental disorders, and persistent family conflict. Some of these items were also assessed in the CIDI, but assessment of adversity in terms of the event and timing of the event was more detailed in the LHC administration.

To assess general family history, substance use and offense history, contacts with services or systems, and social supports, we adapted additional prompts from our previous studies of incarcerated females (DeHart, 2008; DeHart & Moran, in press). Here we focus on substance use and offenses including alcohol and drug use; running away; shoplifting, stealing, burglary, or fraud; fighting or physical assault; using weapons or getting weapons offenses; drug dealing or drug offenses; driving under the influence or under suspension; and commercial sex work or trading sex for food, shelter, money, or drugs.

Procedures

Procedures for the LHC were very similar to those described for the structured diagnostic interview. Women who completed the structured diagnostic interview were randomly selected to complete the LHC, with selection limited to post-conviction women at three sites.

Analyses

LHC Survival analyses & Cox regression.

Quantitative LHC data were analyzed using life tables and survival analysis to elucidate patterns of offending over the lifespan. In this type of analysis, the baseline hazard function describes a pattern of risk over time and indicates when a target event (e.g., first use of a weapon) is most likely to occur. Examining the hazard function and isolating time periods with steep slopes is a way to identify risky times during which prevention or risk reduction may take on heightened importance. Hazard and survival plots for different groups (e.g., women with and without SMI) or events (e.g., drug dealing versus commercial sex work) may be compared. Hazard rates provide insight into probability of events over time.

To examine effects of covariates on risk trajectories for crime, we used Cox regression—this approach models the conditional probability of an event as a function of one or more covariates (e.g., commercial sex work as a function of childhood victimization) which are assumed to affect the underlying hazard multiplicatively (proportional across time). Singer and Willett (1991) characterize the hazard model as "a powerful, flexible, and sensitive approach" for analysis of timing of events (p. 279), offering great potential for examining women's pathways to jail. For these analyses, we examine role of factors including SMI, substance use disorder, PTSD, various types of victimization, and childhood non-victimization adversity.

LHC qualitative analyses.

LHC interviews were transribed by each interviewer shortly after completing the interview, utilizing the completed calendar and field notes. Qualitative LHC transcripts were coded and analyzed using MaxQDA software (VERBI GmbH Berlin, Germany). The qualitative software allows the researcher to mark computerized text passages and tag those passages with commentary or codes (e.g., "intimate partner violence"). Codes may be organized into hierarchies, and participant files can be grouped into "families" or categories (e.g., "women with SMI"). For purposes of the present report, we used a first-cycle coding method with provisional top-down coding based on categories of items in women's interviews. This approach allowed us to identify specific exemplars to illustrate findings revealed in quantitative analysis of interview data. In this way, we will bring MaxQDA's powerful capabilities to bear upon inferences as these emerge from the quantitative data, and we will use excerpted segments of women's narratives to elucidate the manifest associations between variables.

Results

Prevalence of mental health problems, offending and victimization in the LHC subsample

As noted above, LHC participants were a subsample ($N = 115$) of the participants who participated in the structured diagnostic interviews ($N = 491$). These participants' rates of mental health problems were similar to those of the full sample. Table 10 illustrates the similarity in prevalence rates of the assessed disorders for the full sample and subsample.

Table 10

Prevalence of Lifetime Disorders in Full Sample and Subsample

Type of lifetime disorder	Full sample % ($N = 491$)	LHC subsample % ($N = 115$)
Serious mental illness	43	50
PTSD	53	51
SUD	82	85

Victimization and offending were assessed in greater detail in the LHC interview. Participants reported on a range of criminal behaviors, not just those they with which they had been charged or convicted. Nearly three-quarters of the women reported committing property offenses (shoplifting, stealing, burglary, or fraud, see Table 11).

Table 11

Prevalence of Self-Reported Lifetime Offending for LHC Participants

Type of offense	Percent of sample ($N = 115$)
Running away (prior to age 18)	43
Fighting or physical assault	56
Shoplifting, stealing, burglary, or fraud	75
Carrying weapons or weapons offenses	33
Dealing drugs or getting drug charges	64
Driving under the influence or under suspension	38
Commercial sex work or trading sex	40

Over half of the women reported dealing drugs or drug charges and fighting or physical assault, and over a third reported running away, carrying weapons, driving under the influence, or commercial sex work. As we will demonstrate in later regression analyses, these offenses often related to women's victimization, substance use, or mental health.

Participants also described a broad range of victimization experiences across their lifetimes. As illustrated in Table 12, sexual violence was experienced by an overwhelming majority of women in the subsample, with rates being particularly high for molestation by an adult prior to age 16 as well as for forcible rape after age 16.

Table 12

Prevalence of Victimization Experiences Described in the LHC Interviews

Women's victimization experiences	Percent of sample (*N* = 115)
Any caregiver violence (prior to age 18)	**60**
Physical abuse	49
Use of weapon	30
Psychological abuse	43
Neglect	20
Parental kidnapping or custodial interference	7
Any partner violence	**77**
Physical abuse	71
Use of weapon	48
Partner rape	24
Any non-familial violence	**63**
Gang or group attack	13
Stranger/acquaintance attack	21
Stranger/acquaintance use of weapon	22
Bullying or harassment	47
Any sexual violence	**86**
Molestation by adult (prior to age 16)	48
Molestation by peers (prior to age 16)	25
Statutory rape (prior to age 16)	21
Partner rape (age 16 or older)	24
Other forcible rape (age 16 or older)	39
Alcohol/drug-enabled sexual assault	21
Any witnessed violence	**73**
Witnessed caregiver violence	45
Witnessed a bad attack	46
Witnessed a murder or dead body	40

In fact, sexual victimization of any given type (e.g., statutory rape, partner rape, drug-facilitated assaults) was reported by no fewer than one in five women. Intimate partner violence—

particularly physical abuse—was also exceedingly common. Women also frequently experienced child physical and psychological abuse as well as witnessing violence in their homes and communities. Non-familial/non-intimate attacks were predominated by bullying or harassment, although about one in five women experienced major assaults by strangers or acquaintances. As we will illustrate through regression analyses, various types of victimization were related to women's offending patterns.

Risk Trajectories for Substance Use & Offending

Actuarial life tables were generated to examine overall risk for substance use and different types of offending across the lifespan. Figures 6 through 13 display hazard functions for the onset of various offenses, illustrating highest-risk time periods for onset of substance use and offending. These hazard functions depict the instantaneous rate of experiencing the event in question (e.g., onset of substance use) among cases who have arrived at that time interval without experiencing the event (survival). The value of a hazard function cannot be lower than zero, but can exceed 1, thus does not represent a probability, but rather represents a rate of failures (occurrence of the modeled outcome). However, knowing something about the relationship between "failures" (those who experience the event) and "survivors" (those who do not) provides insight into risk, with steep hazard functions being indicative of the "riskiness" of a particular time period. Because calculation of the hazard rate at each step or time period contains fewer cases than the calculation at the previous step (because those who experienced the event or "aged out" are removed from the risk set), estimates at later times are more variable than those based on a greater number of cases.

Each figure also shows the median age until onset for each behavior (i.e., age by which 50% of the sample had engaged in the behavior). This elucidates which behaviors might be characterized by earlier versus later onsets. Figures are provided for behaviors including substance use, running away, property offending, fighting or physical assault, weapons use, drug dealing/charges, driving under the influence, and commercial sex work.

Onset of substance abuse.

As illustrated in Figure 6, about half of the women in the subsample had begun using alcohol and/or drugs before they reached 16 years of age. A sizable number of women (n = 18) began using substances by age 11, and risk increased sharply when they reached the 12-15 year age range.

Figure 6. Interpolated Actuarial Hazard Function for Onset of Substance Use

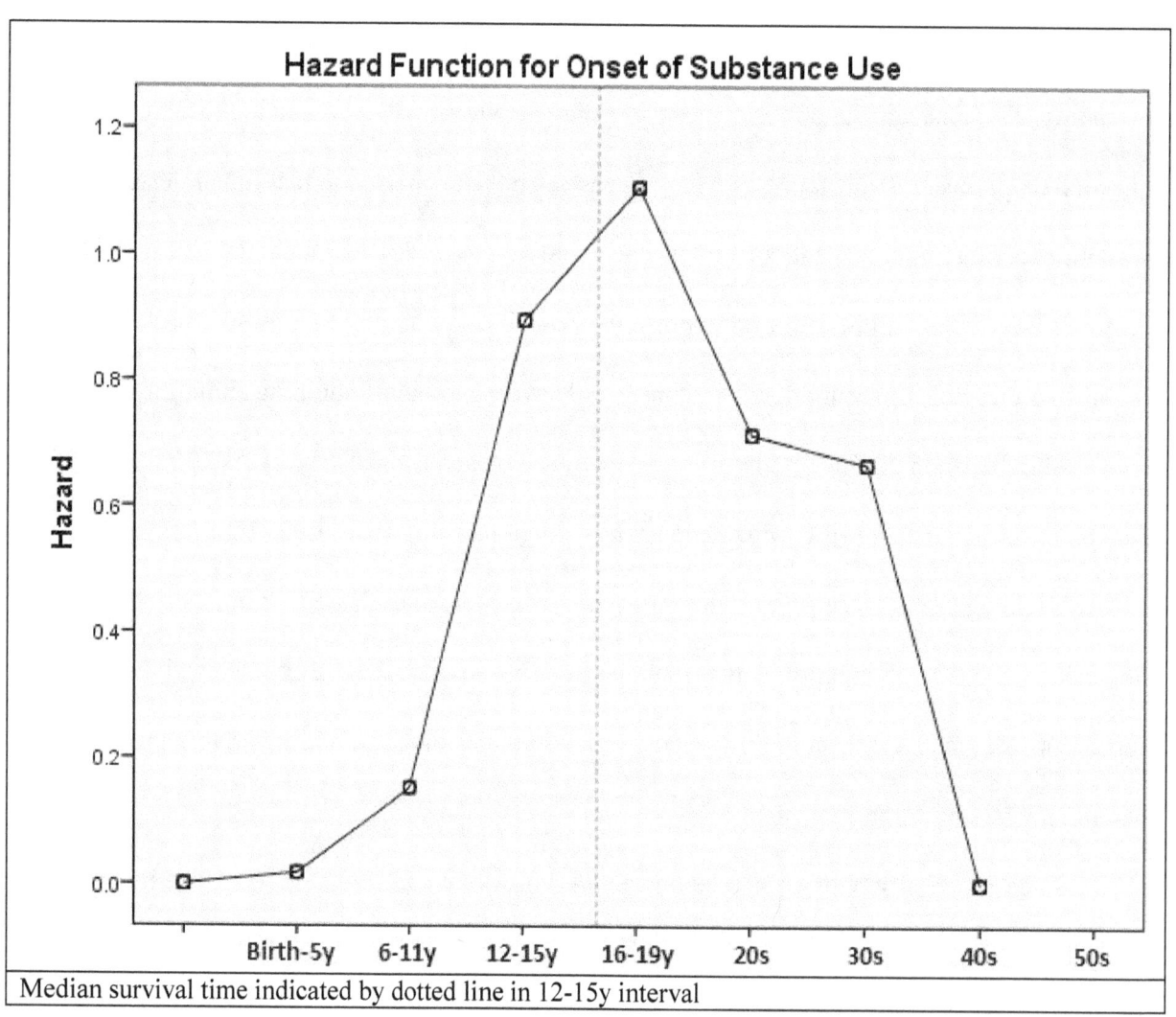

#Entering	115	115	113	97	37	10	4	2
#Onset	0	2	16	60	26	5	2	0
#Age out	0	0	0	0	1	1	0	2

After this, a majority of those who had not begun using substances began to do so. A few of the remaining women began using substances in their twenties and thirties, but risk diminished by the time women reached their forties.

Figure 7. Interpolated Actuarial Hazard Function for Onset of Running Away

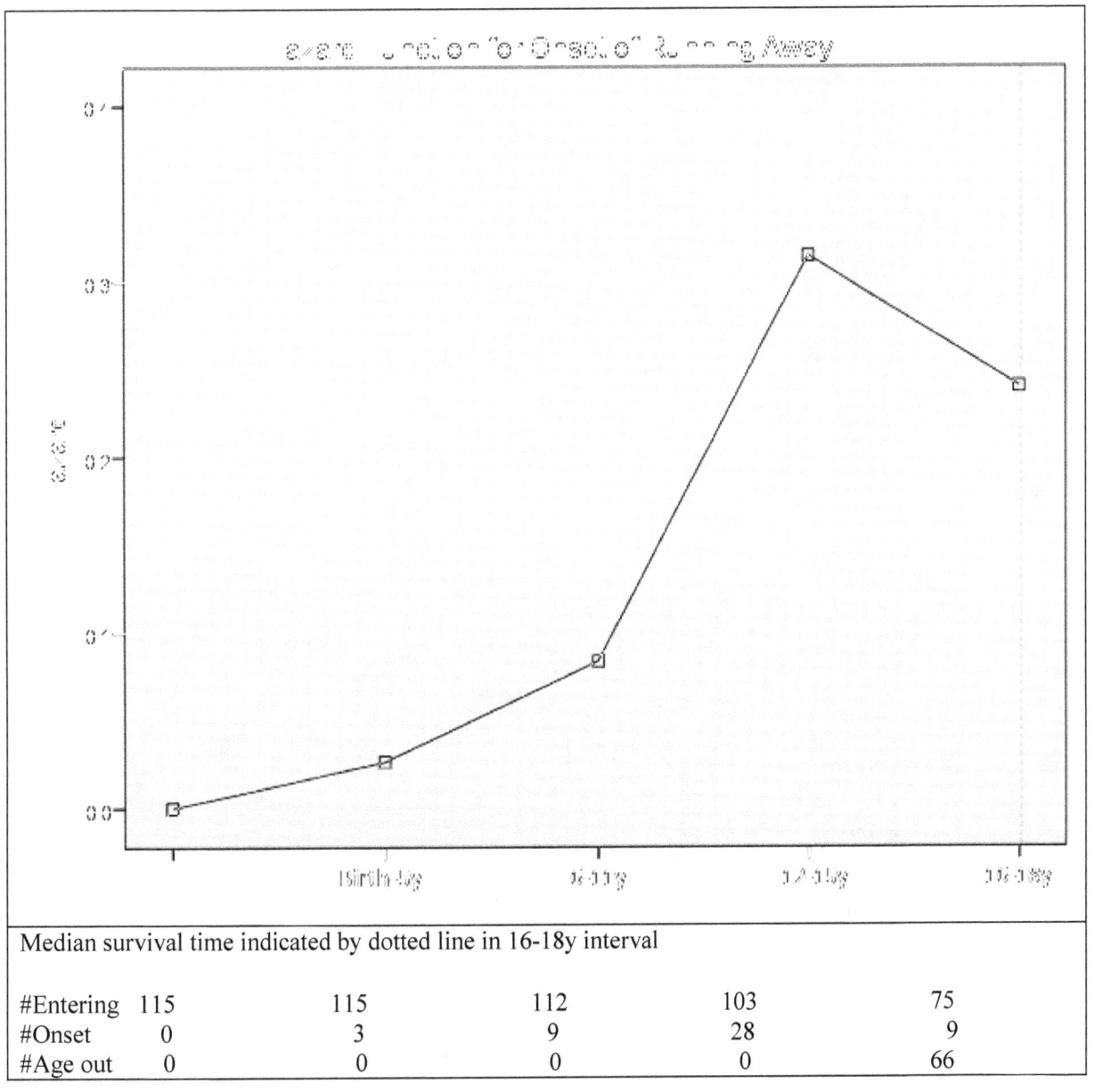

Median survival time indicated by dotted line in 16-18y interval

#Entering	115	115	112	103	75
#Onset	0	3	9	28	9
#Age out	0	0	0	0	66

Onset of running away.

As can be inferred from the median in Figure 7, a slight majority of the women in our subsample had never run away as youth. Of those who did run away, over a third did so by the time they reached 11 years of age. But, as indicated by the steep slope after this period, the highest risk period for running away occurred in the 12-15 year age range. Risk declined somewhat as the women reached their late teens.

Figure 8. Interpolated Actuarial Hazard Function for Onset of Fighting or Physical Assault

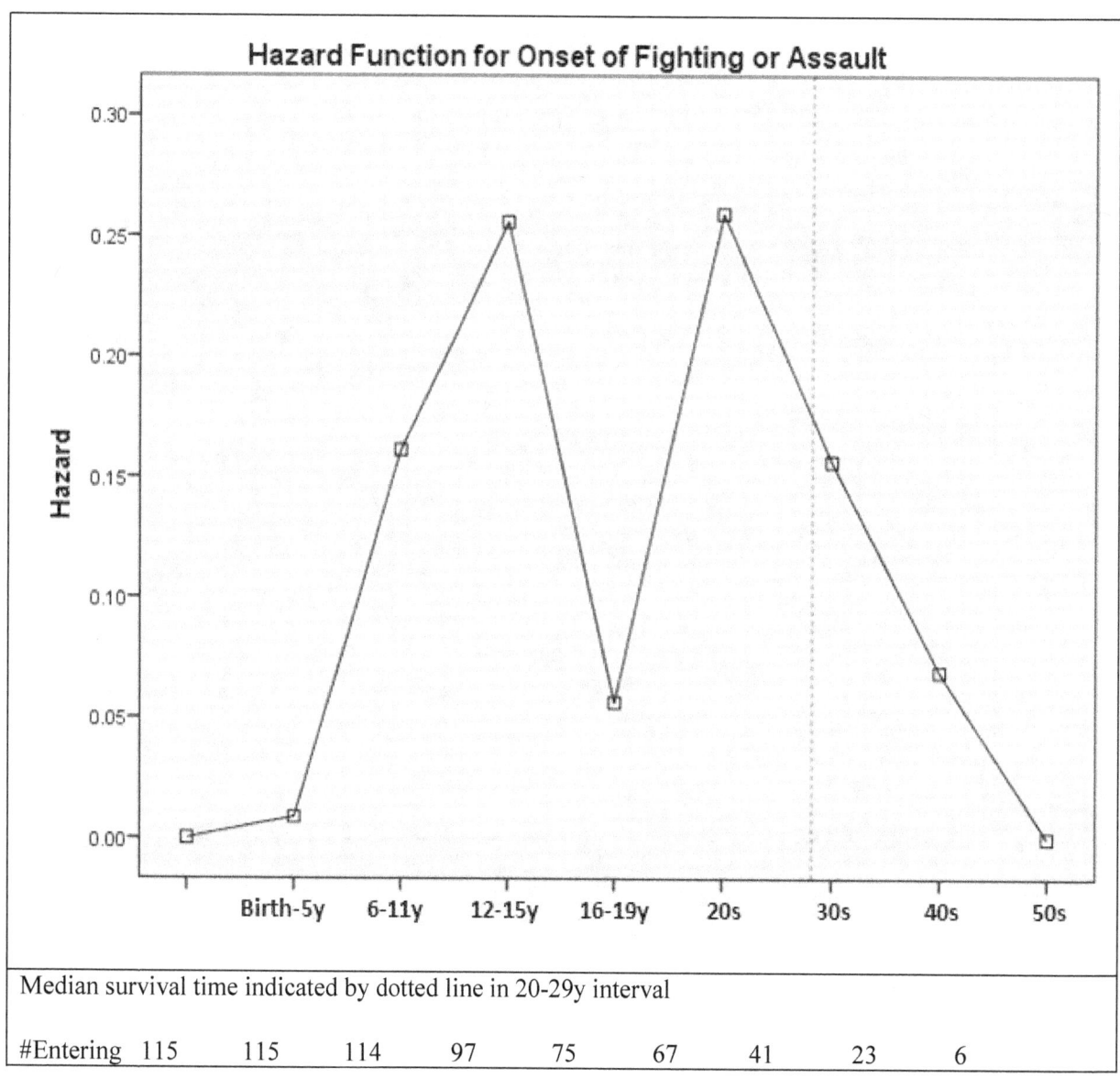

Median survival time indicated by dotted line in 20-29y interval								
#Entering 115	115	114	97	75	67	41	23	6

#Onset	0	1	17	22	4	14	5	1	0
#Age out	0	0	0	0	4	12	13	16	6

Onset of fighting or physical assault.

Figure 8 shows the "twin peaked" pattern of risk for onset of fighting or physical assault. As can be seen by the median, about half of the LHC participants had physically fought or assaulted someone before they reached their thirties. Onset for fighting often began in childhood or early adolescence (the first peak), after which risk drops drastically for persons in their late teens. Risk peaks for the remaining women in their twenties (second peak), steadily declining thereafter.

Onset of property crimes.

Aside from substance use, property crimes appear to be one of the earlier-onset crimes for the women. Half of the women who completed the LHC interview reported that they engaged in some form of property offending before reaching their twenties. As illustrated in Figure 9, risk sharply rises in pre-pubescence, with gradual increases through the women's twenties. Risk drops somewhat in women's thirties, but there is another peak for the few remaining women in their forties. Examining specific cases through women's qualitative narratives uncovers that much of the earlier-onset risk is attributable to shoplifting or burglary, while later-onset property crimes often involve things such as check-cashing schemes or embezzling.

Onset of weapons use.

As can be inferred from Figure 10, carrying or selling weapons or being charged with weapons offenses was one of the less common offenses described by women in the LHC interview, with fewer than half of women reporting that they had engaged in these offenses before all participants "aged out." Risk for onset of weapons use was fairly steady for women through their teens, twenties, and thirties, with a couple of additional women starting to carry weapons in their forties or fifties. In qualitative accounts, many women described carrying

knives for protection, some women carried guns, and a few became involved in selling weapons.

Figure 9. Interpolated Actuarial Hazard Function for Onset of Property Crimes

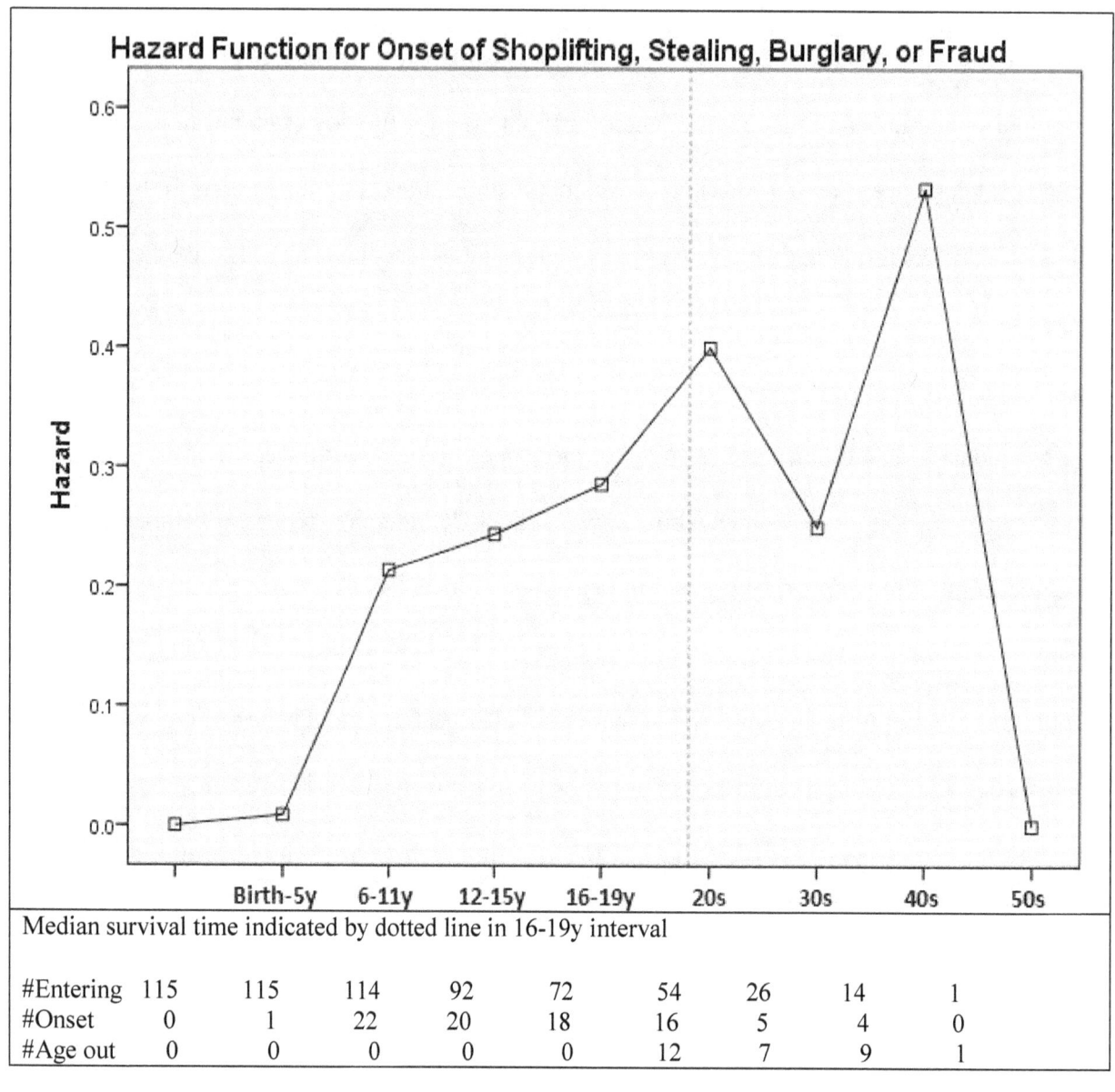

	Birth-5y	6-11y	12-15y	16-19y	20s	30s	40s	50s
Median survival time indicated by dotted line in 16-19y interval								
#Entering	115	115	114	92	72	54	26	14	1
#Onset	0	1	22	20	18	16	5	4	0
#Age out	0	0	0	0	0	12	7	9	1

Figure 10. Interpolated Actuarial Hazard Function for Onset of Weapons Use

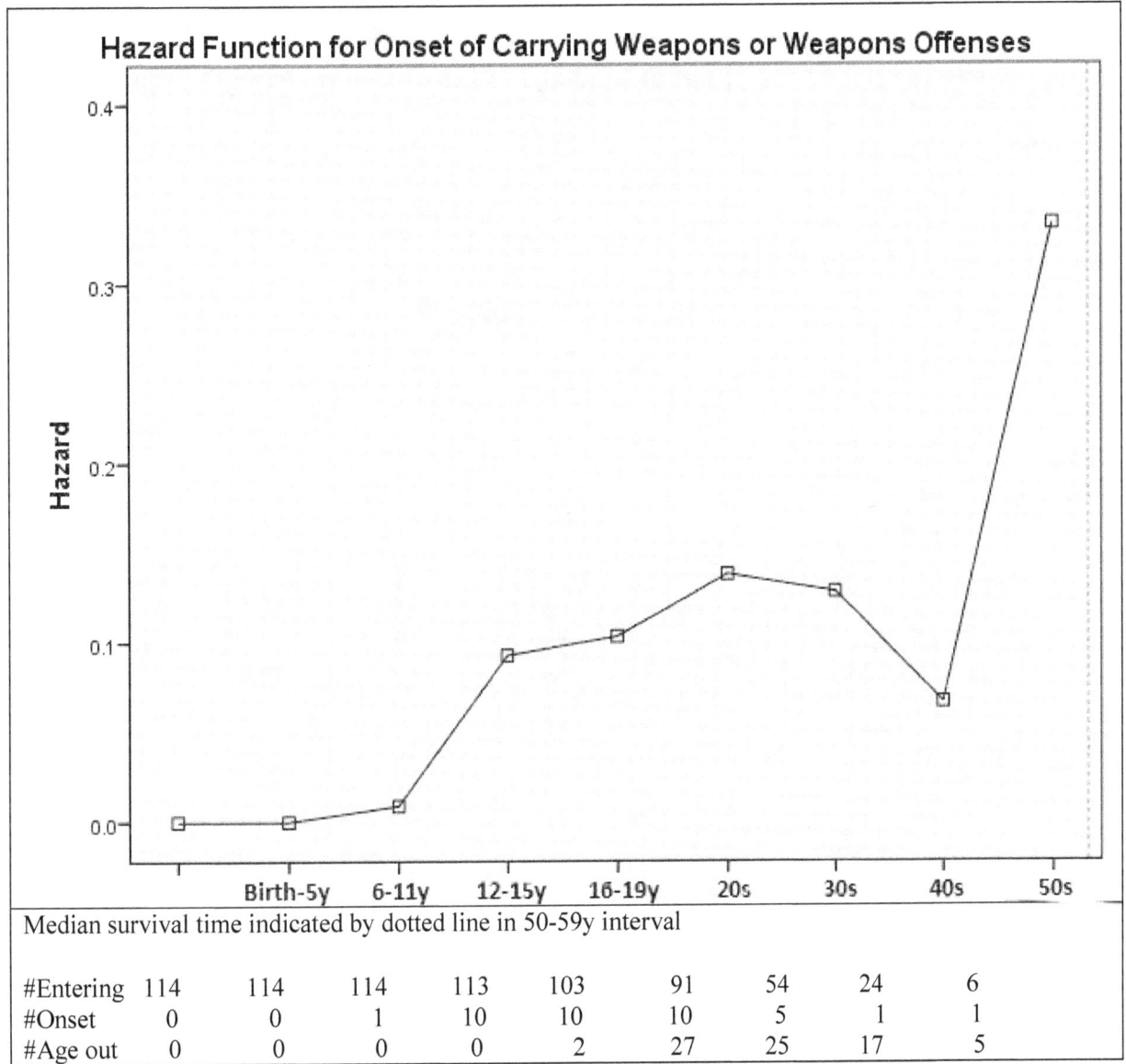

Hazard Function for Onset of Carrying Weapons or Weapons Offenses

Median survival time indicated by dotted line in 50-59y interval

	Birth-5y	6-11y	12-15y	16-19y	20s	30s	40s	50s
#Entering	114	114	114	113	103	91	54	24	6
#Onset	0	0	1	10	10	10	5	1	1
#Age out	0	0	0	0	2	27	25	17	5

Onset of drug dealing/charges.

Figure 11 shows that dealing drugs or getting charged with drug offenses was reported in the teens or twenties by over half of the LHC participants. Onset of such offenses increased progressively from early adolescence through women's twenties, after which risk stabilized through the thirties and forties and dropped off for the few remaining older women.

Figure 11. Interpolated Actuarial Hazard Function for Onset of Drug Dealing/Charges

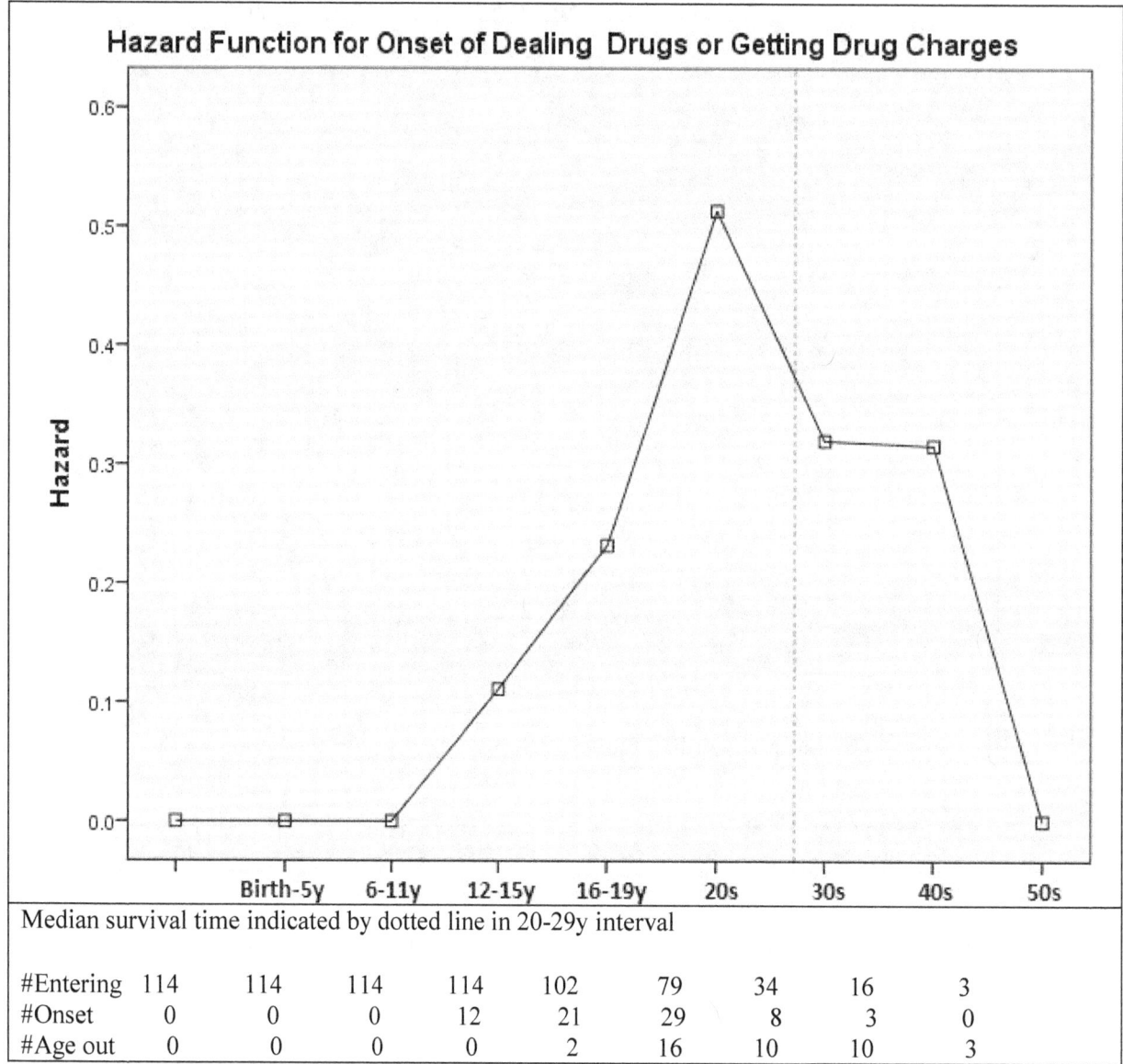

	Birth-5y	6-11y	12-15y	16-19y	20s	30s	40s	50s
Median survival time indicated by dotted line in 20-29y interval								
#Entering	114	114	114	114	102	79	34	16	3
#Onset	0	0	0	12	21	29	8	3	0
#Age out	0	0	0	0	2	16	10	10	3

Onset of driving under the influence or under suspension.

Nearly half of the LHC participants had been arrested for driving under the influence of alcohol or drugs (DUI) or for driving under suspension or "without privileges" (DUS). DUI was by far the more common offense, and, as illustrated in Figure 12, onset typically began in the late teens, with risk peaking in the twenties and thirties, and declining sharply thereafter.

Figure 12. Interpolated Actuarial Hazard Function for Onset of DUI/DUS

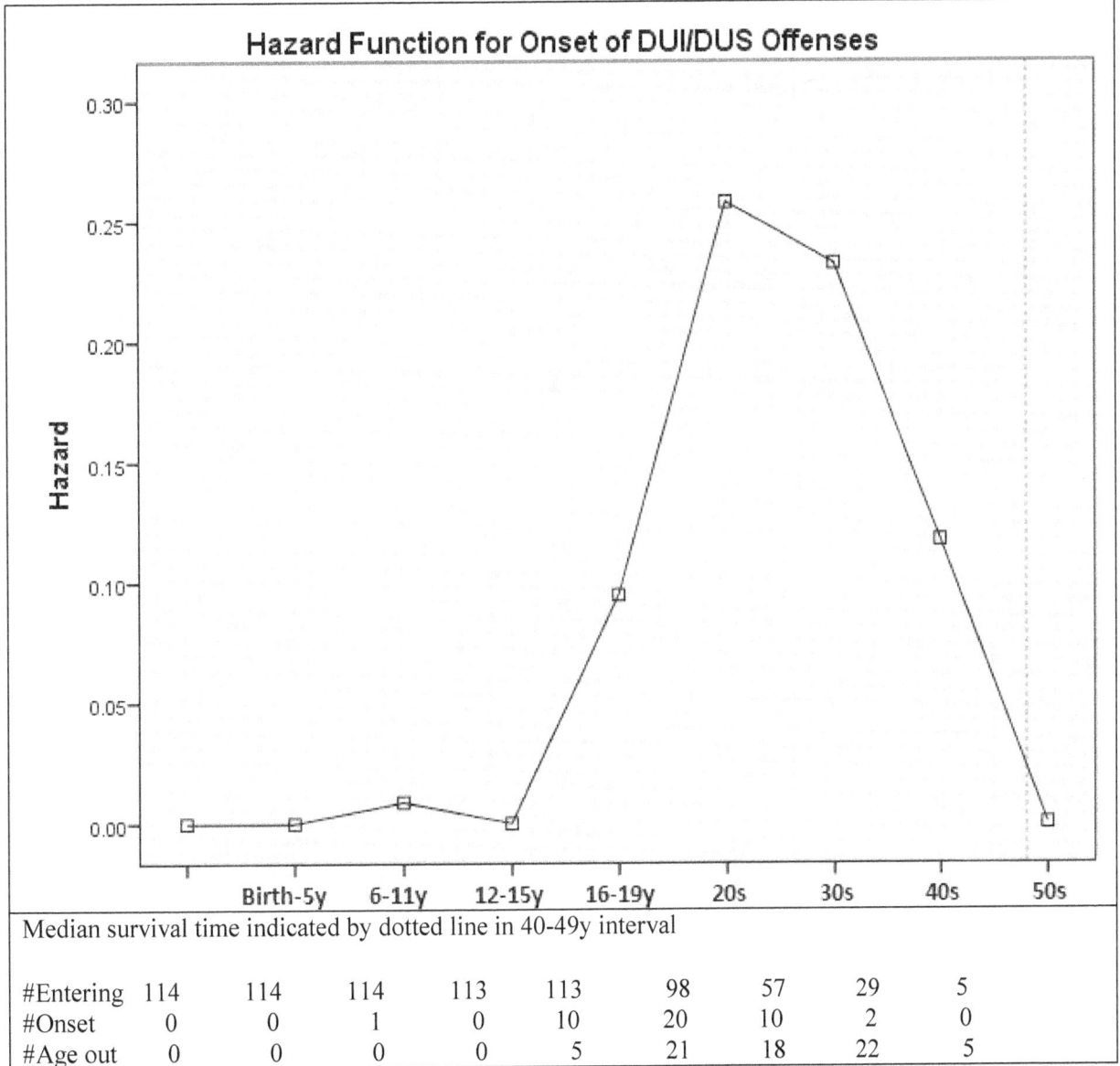

Median survival time indicated by dotted line in 40-49y interval

	Birth-5y	6-11y	12-15y	16-19y	20s	30s	40s	50s
#Entering	114	114	114	113	113	98	57	29	5
#Onset	0	0	1	0	10	20	10	2	0
#Age out	0	0	0	0	5	21	18	22	5

Onset of sex work.

As Figure 13 indicates, fewer than half of the LHC participants had engaged in commercial sex or traded sex for food, shelter, drugs, or money before "aging out" of the risk set. Although a few women reported trading sex in pubescence or early adolescence, onset more typically occurred in the late teens or twenties. Some women became involved in the sex trade in their thirties, and one woman did so in her fifties. The latter case was particularly tragic, as the woman describes how her desperation for drugs drove her to the street even after being stabbed by a "john."

> *#43030 That whole thing should have been a wake-up call but it wasn't. She still continued to get high. She went out with staples in her stomach and walked the same street. She ran into that same guy again.*

Figure 13. Interpolated Actuarial Hazard Function for Onset of Sex Work

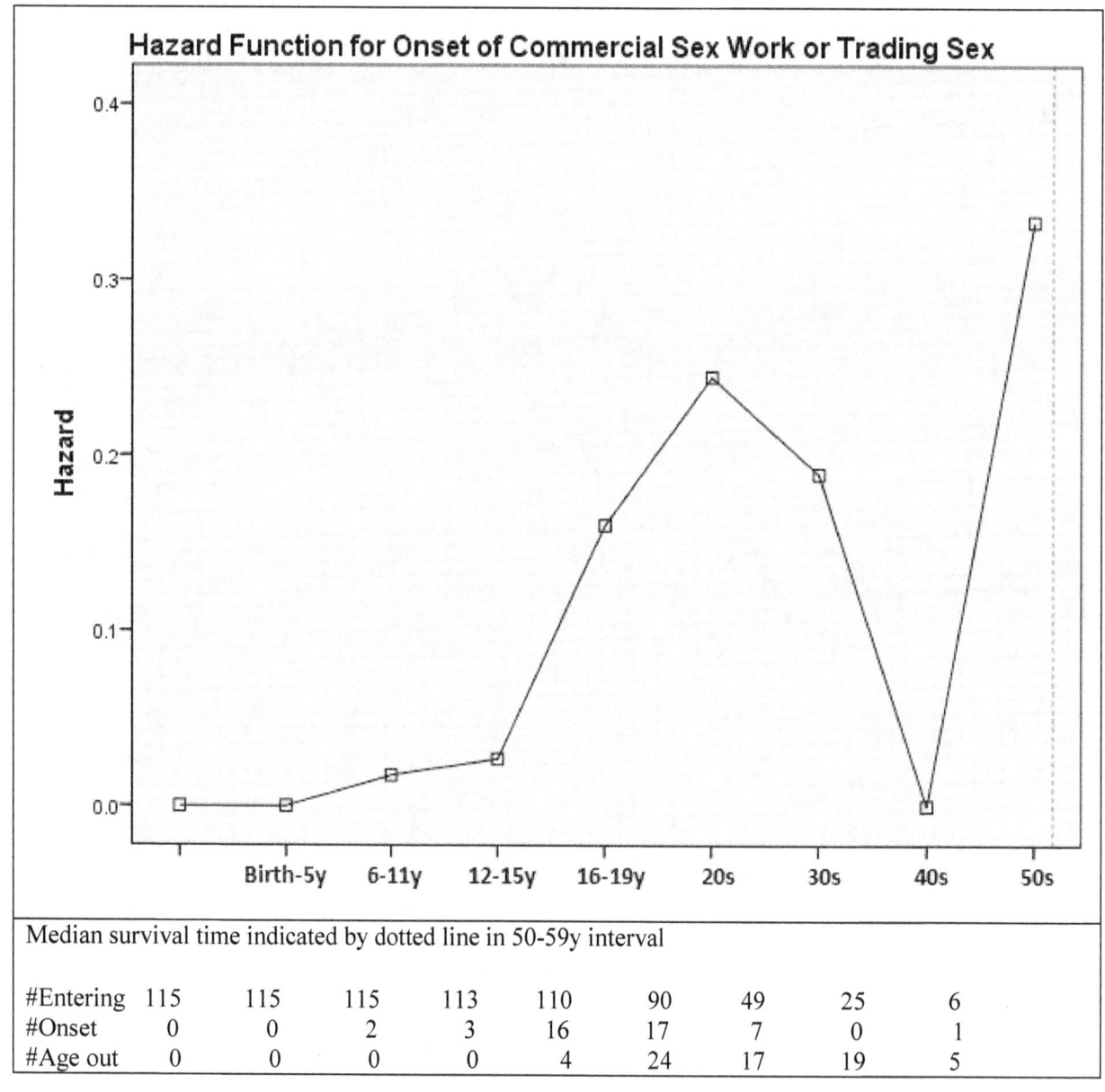

Median survival time indicated by dotted line in 50-59y interval								
#Entering	115	115	115	113	110	90	49	25	6
#Onset	0	0	2	3	16	17	7	0	1
#Age out	0	0	0	0	4	24	17	19	5

Relationship of Mental Health, Trauma, and Adversity to Substance Use & Offending

Model building & stratification by mental health status.

For the following analyses, Cox regression was used to examine association of mental health, trauma, and adversity to onset of offending. Preliminary analyses of actuarial survival functions indicated significant differences between persons with and without mental illness for survival of substance use ($\chi^2 = 9.74$), running away ($\chi^2 = 4.68$), and drug dealing/offenses ($\chi^2 = 3.99$), $ps < .05$, as well as trends for fighting or physical assault ($\chi^2 = 3.03$) and property crimes ($\chi^2 = 2.59$), $dfs = 1$, N = 115, $ps < .10$. Women's narratives indicated that mental health issues such as depression often stemmed from experiences of victimization or loss and were intertwined with women's use of drugs and violence.

> *#32029 She reports that mental health problems have affected her life a lot. She saw her first counselor when her daughter died in the fire....[Describing her own physical and psychological victimization in childhood and adulthood], she states that she was not hurt so much physically but was always hurt more by verbal and mental abuse. The slaps and punches go away but the "words and verbal abuse leave permanent scars in your mind." She is now on meds for anxiety, panic attacks. She also had these problems when she was out of jail, but self-medicated with Percocet, Morphine pills and Benadryl.*

> *#32107 She and her sister were molested by their grandfather starting with the time she was 10 until about 13....When she was 27, she slashed her grandfather's tires. She also smashed his windows and went in to talk to him, to see if he'd changed. She didn't get a "sorry" out of him—just excuses—so she slapped him....Here in jail, she feels she needs medication but isn't getting it. The other day, she got so angry that she punched another inmate without being able to control it.*

Given the difference in baseline hazards for those with and without SMI, we chose to stratify by SMI. This allows examination of distinct patterns of risk. Each of the following Cox regression equations includes time-to-onset of substance use or offending as the dependent variable, SMI as the stratification variable, and independent variables including indicators of substance use disorder, PTSD, caregiver violence, partner violence, non-familial violence, sexual violence, witnessing violence, and childhood non-victimization adversity. Forward stepwise entry with an entry criterion of $p < .05$ was used for covariates, and Peto-Breslow's estimation of the baseline hazard adjusts for ties.

Onset of substance use.

Women with SMI had elevated risk for onset of substance use across the lifespan (see Figure 14). Of covariates, only substance use disorder was a significant predictor of onset. The hazard ratio indicates that women with substance use disorder (SUD) were at more than twice the risk for onset of substance use relative to those who did not meet SUD diagnostic criteria.

Onset of running away.

As illustrated in Figure 15 women with SMI had elevated risk for running away in their teens. Caregiver violence (e.g., physical and psychological abuse, neglect, or parental kidnapping) was a significant predictor of the first time women ran away. Women's qualitative accounts support these quantitative findings, as women often described running away as a means of ending abuse from caregivers.

> *#31018 Her mom abused her until she was 14 and ran away. When she was 11, her mom started punching her….Her mom hit her with extension cords—whatever—hangers, belts. And her mom also called her names and said mean things to her the whole time. There was a lot of neglect. They didn't go to the doctor for stuff, they just had to deal with it.*

The hazard ratio indicates that women who experienced caregiver violence were almost nine times as likely to run away in their teens relative to those who did not experience such maltreatment.

Figure 14. Interpolated Hazard at the Mean of Covariates for Onset of Substance Use

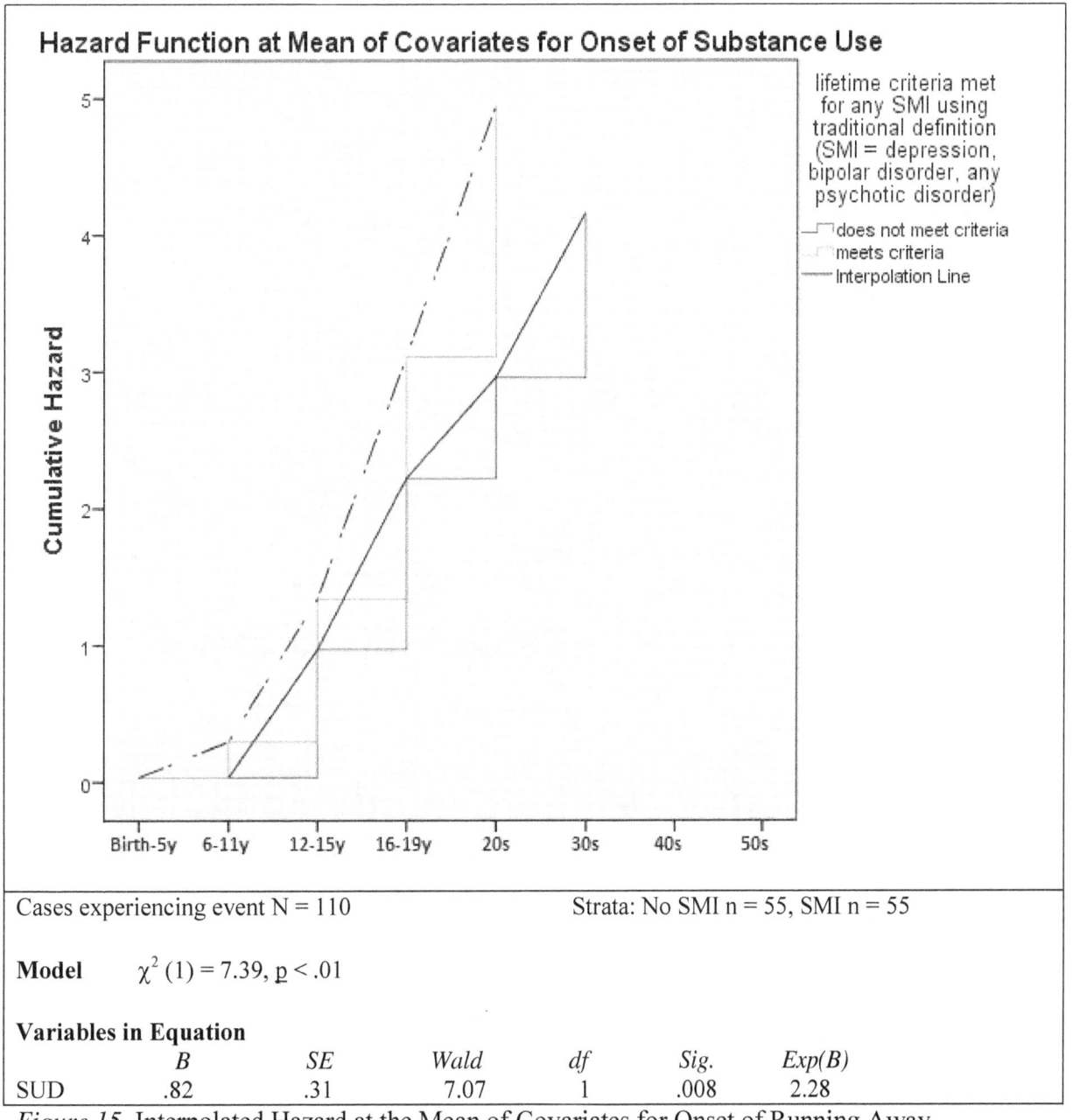

Cases experiencing event N = 110			Strata: No SMI n = 55, SMI n = 55		

Model $\chi^2 (1) = 7.39, p < .01$

Variables in Equation

	B	SE	Wald	df	Sig.	Exp(B)
SUD	.82	.31	7.07	1	.008	2.28

Figure 15. Interpolated Hazard at the Mean of Covariates for Onset of Running Away

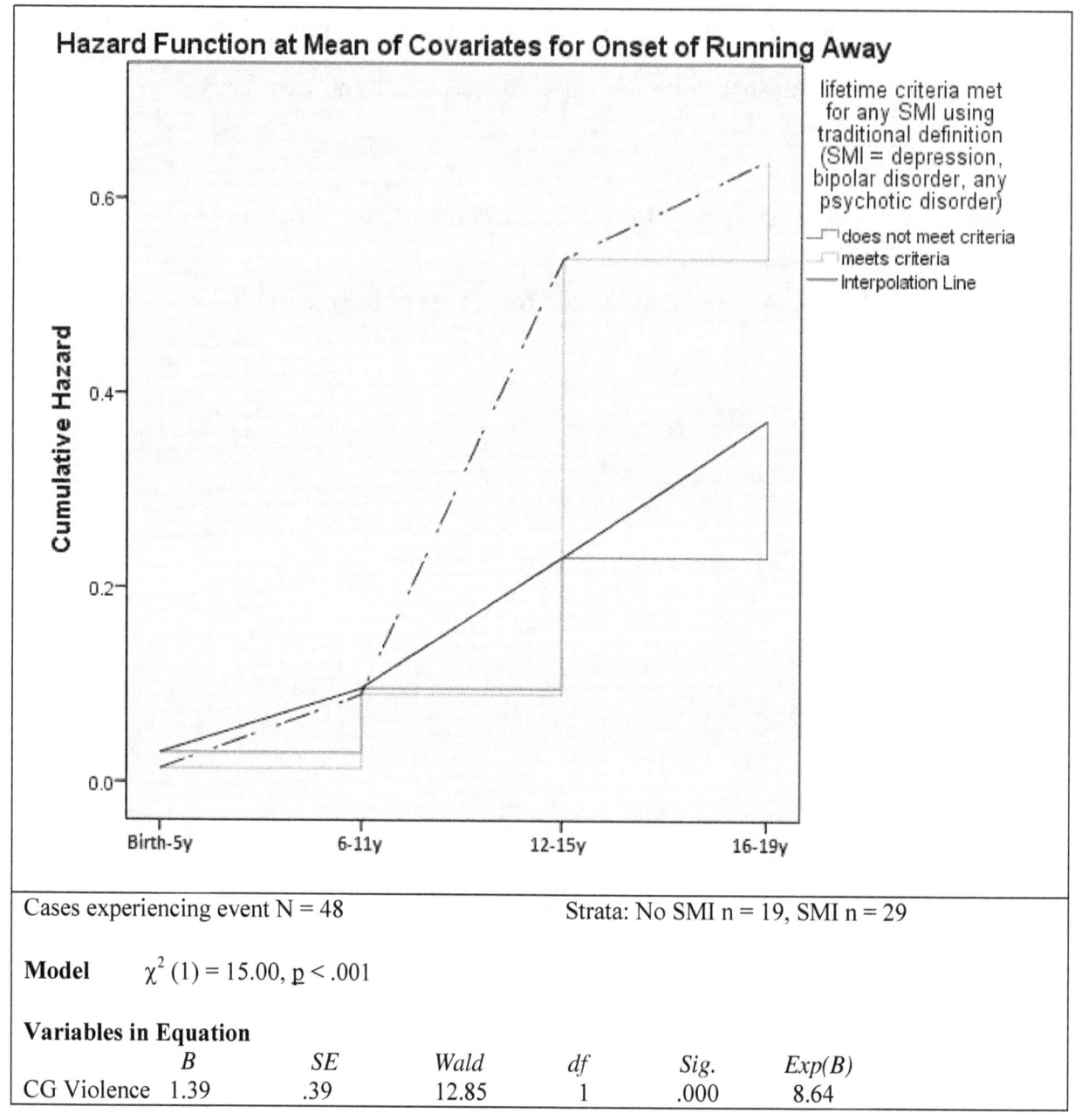

Cases experiencing event N = 48			**Strata: No SMI n = 19, SMI n = 29**		
Model χ^2 (1) = 15.00, p < .001					
Variables in Equation					
	B	*SE*	*Wald*	*df*	*Sig.*	*Exp(B)*
CG Violence	1.39	.39	12.85	1	.000	8.64

Onset of fighting or physical assault.

As illustrated in Figure 16, women with SMI had elevated risk for fighting and/or

engaging in physical assault throughout their lifespan. Witnessing violence in their homes or

communities was a significant predictor of onset. Women's narratives revealed that women's fighting and assaults were frequently responses to witnessed violence in their homes and communities, as in the following account:

> *#11046 She once had a physical altercation with her brother because he was beating their grandmother. She hit him with a lamp. It was better that her brother fight with her than with her grandmother. She thinks her brother was abusive because of how their grandfather behaved and messed them all up.*

The hazard ratio indicates that women who witnessed violence were almost twice as likely to engage in fighting or physical assaults.

Onset of property crimes.

Women with SMI also had elevated risk for property crime (e.g., shoplifting, stealing, burglary, fraud) across the lifespan (see Figure 17). Witnessing violence was a significant predictor of onset. Examination of women's narratives did not reveal overt links between witnessing violence and committing property crimes. However, examination of specific cases revealed that both factors often co-existed in criminally involved family or social networks. This is exemplified by the statement of one active shoplifter:

> *#24088 She says that being physically violent is the norm for the people she does drugs with. People become high and argue over small things.*

Hazard ratios indicate that women who witnessed violence in their homes or communities were at twice the risk of those who did not for engaging in property crime.

Figure 16. Interpolated Hazard at the Mean of Covariates for Onset of Fighting/Assault

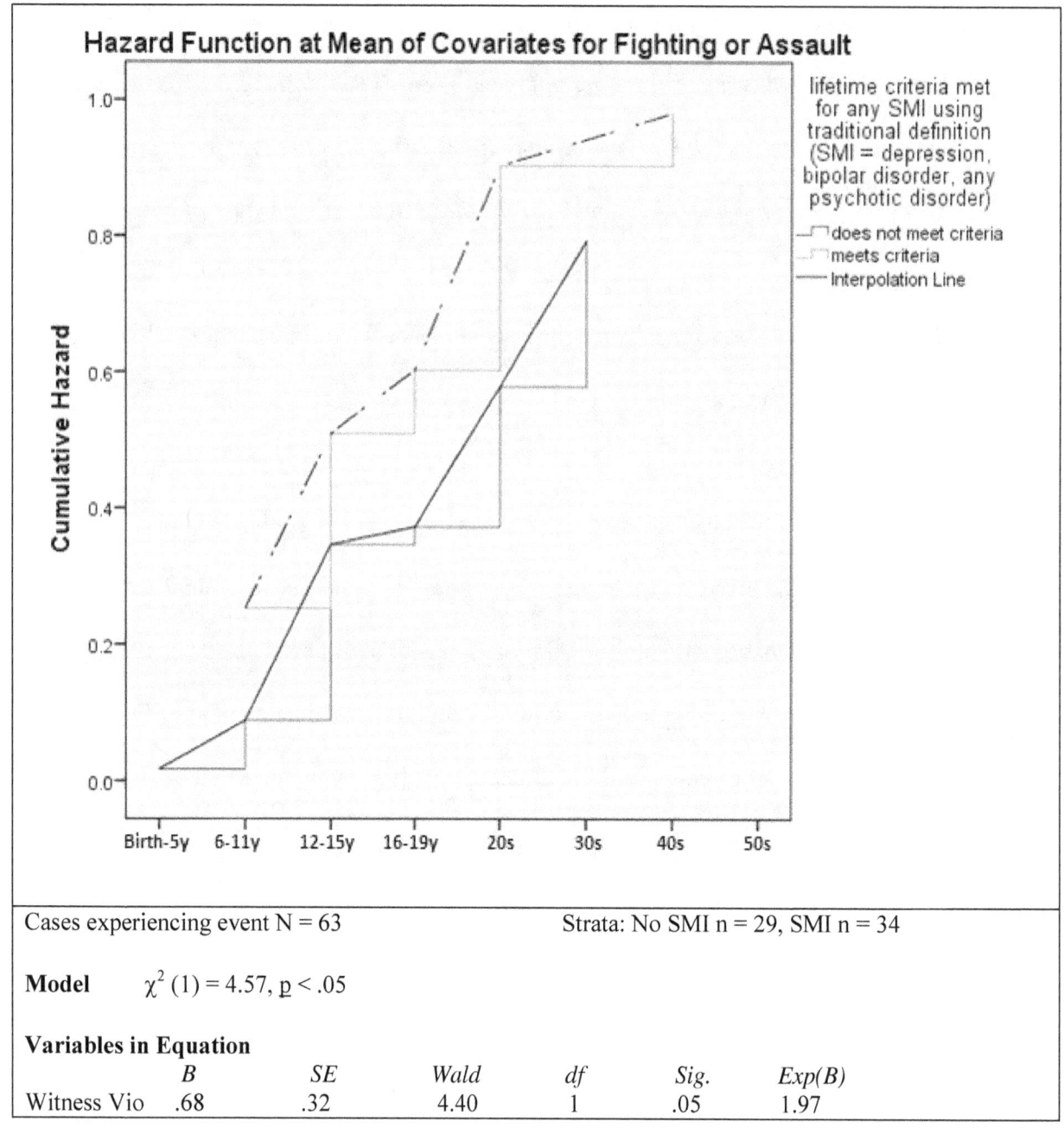

Cases experiencing event N = 63	Strata: No SMI n = 29, SMI n = 34

Model $\chi^2 (1) = 4.57$, p $< .05$

Variables in Equation

	B	SE	Wald	df	Sig.	Exp(B)
Witness Vio	.68	.32	4.40	1	.05	1.97

Figure 17. Interpolated Hazard at the Mean of Covariates for Onset of Property Crimes

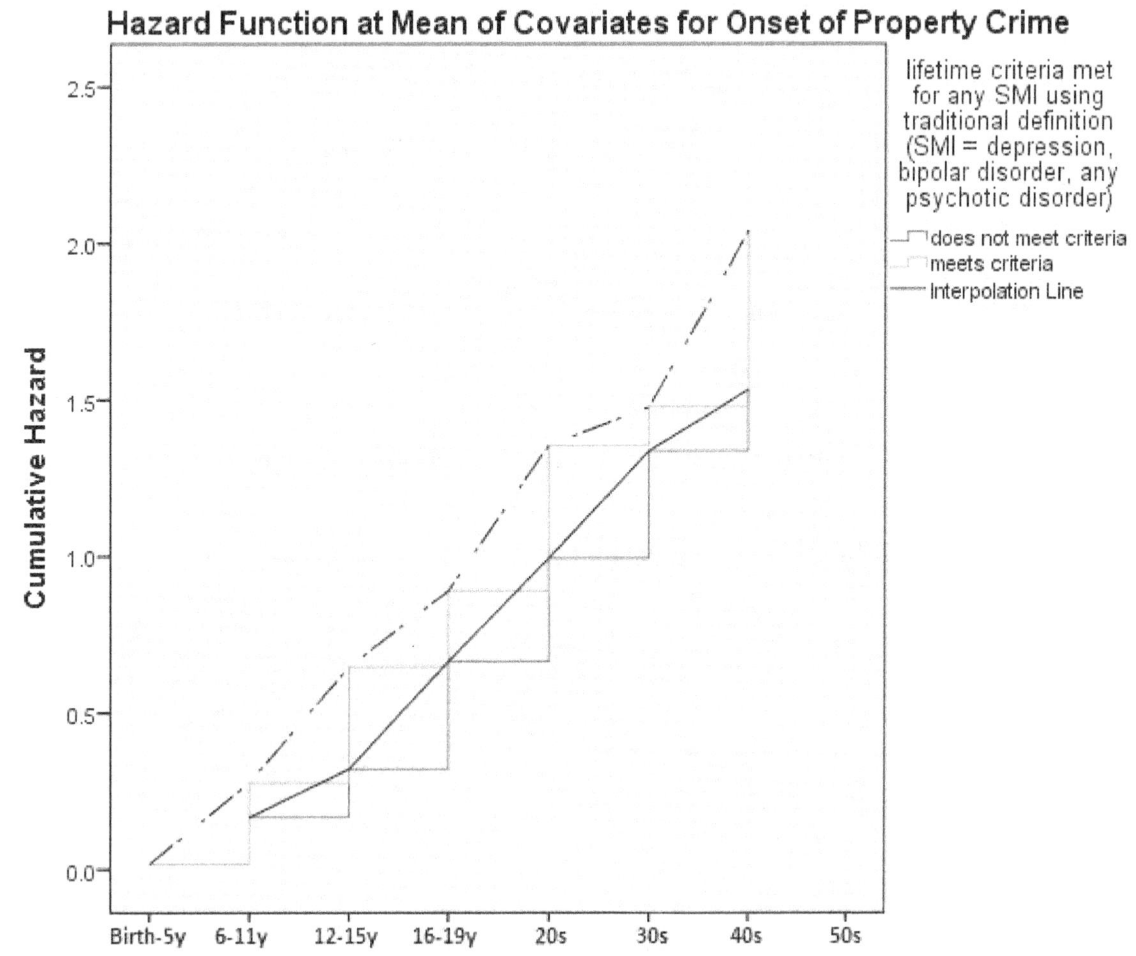

Cases experiencing event N = 86			Strata: No SMI n = 41, SMI n = 45		

Model $\chi^2 (1) = 7.27, \underline{p} < .01$

Variables in Equation

	B	*SE*	*Wald*	*df*	*Sig.*	*Exp(B)*
Witness Vio	.70	.26	7.01	1	.008	2.01

Onset of weapons use.

Recall that our preliminary analyses did not reveal differences in risk for weapons use among women with SMI and those who did not meet diagnostic criteria. As illustrated in Figure 18, witnessing violence was a significant predictor of onset of weapons use. Most commonly, women described carrying weapons in a protective manner, often as a result of witnessed violence or social norms in "rough" neighborhoods:

> *#42012 She carried a knife in high school. That was back in the day when everybody carried one. Back then, children were not using guns. They would have fistfights, carry around box cutters.*

The hazard ratio indicates that women who witnessed violence were almost eight times as likely to use a weapon.

Figure 18. Interpolated Hazard at the Mean of Covariates for Onset of Weapons Use

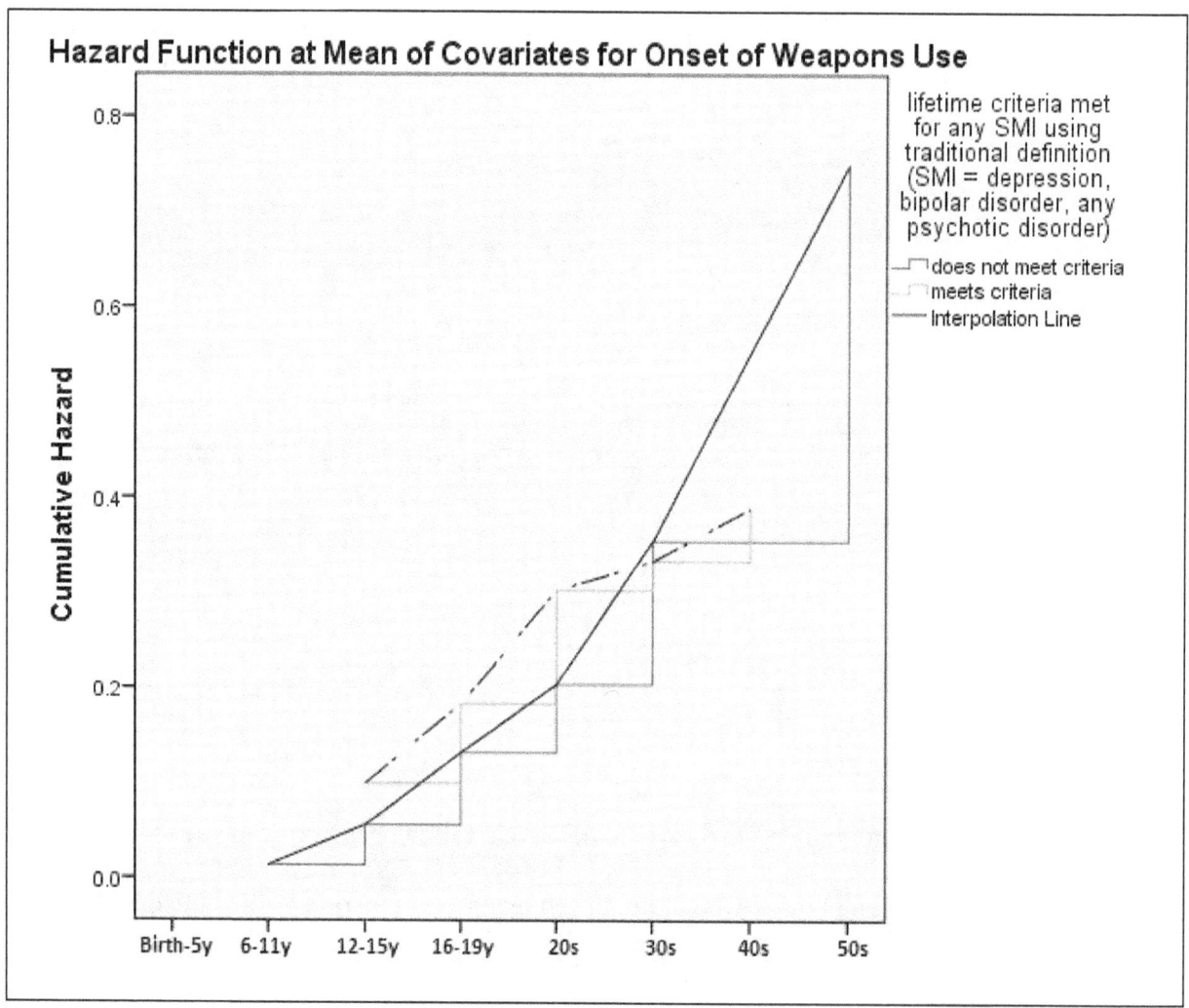

Cases experiencing event N = 38			Strata: No SMI n = 18, SMI n = 20		
Model χ^2 (1) = 11.28, $\underline{p}$ < .001					
Variables in Equation					
B	*SE*	*Wald*	*df*	*Sig.*	*Exp(B)*
Witness Vio 2.06	.72	8.03	1	.000	7.86

Onset of drug dealing/charges.

Women with SMI had elevated risk for dealing drugs or getting charged with drug offenses (see Figure 19). Partner violence was a significant predictor of onset of such drug offenses. Although coercion to sell or use drugs was present in some women's stories, more commonly the women described violent men as their co-offenders in the drug trade:

#32039 Her husband M was nice in the beginning. She loved him. When they were using together, it turned awful....he got out of prison and they started selling dope together because they wanted more money. At 30, she was sending drugs through the mail and just loving the money and all the drugs that go with it. But it was horrible on the streets. They had to rob and steal. M carried a gun and they robbed people with it. M held out a gun to her about 5 times in their relationship and told her the only reason he didn't shoot her was because she was the mother of his kids. One time, she tried to take the gun away from him and it went off, scraping her foot. They both started laughing about it; they were both high at the time.

The hazard ratio indicates that women who experienced intimate partner violence were more than twice as likely to deal drugs or get charged with drug offenses.

Figure 19. Interpolated Hazard at the Mean of Covariates for Onset of Drug Dealing/Charges

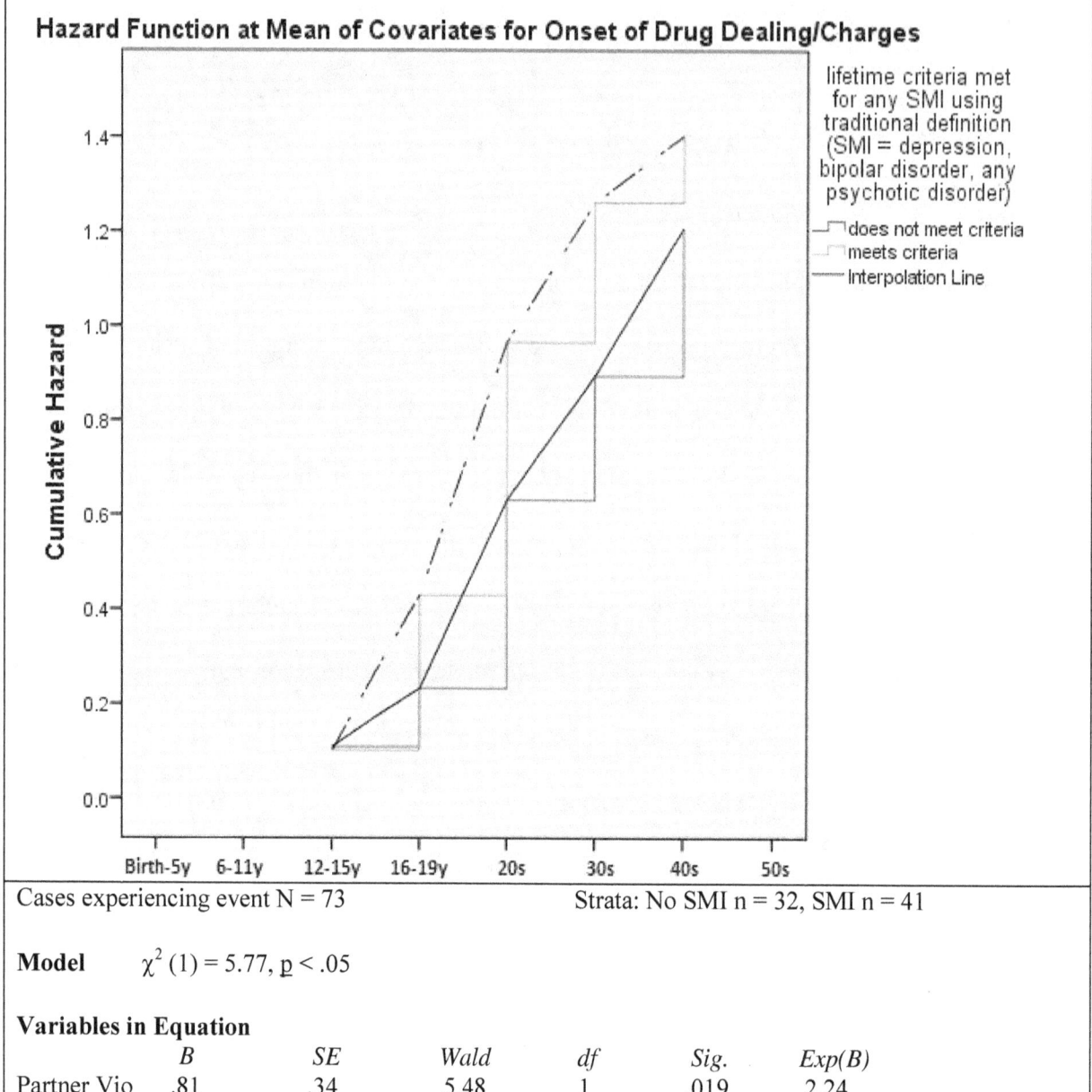

Cases experiencing event N = 73			Strata: No SMI n = 32, SMI n = 41		
Model $\chi^2 (1) = 5.77$, p < .05					
Variables in Equation					
	B	SE	Wald	df	Sig.	Exp(B)
Partner Vio	.81	.34	5.48	1	.019	2.24

Onset of driving under the influence or under suspension.

Recall that risk for driving under the influence or under suspension did not differ for women with and without SMI in our preliminary analyses. Figure 20 shows that only substance use disorder was a significant predictor of onset. The role of substance use disorder in driving under the influence is obvious and is exemplified in women's narratives:

#11002 With her 5th and most recent DUI, she was blacked out. She does remember that she had started to drink in her apartment, and it was St. Patrick's day…. When she woke up in jail, she thought her DUI had been at night, but then found out it had been at 7am….She guesses that she must have woken up and guzzled vodka.

The hazard ratio indicates that women with substance use disorder (SUD) were seven times as likely to drive under the influence or under suspension.

Onset of sex work.

Similarly, risk for sex work did not differ significantly for women with and without SMI in our preliminary analyses. In contrast, as illustrated in Figure 21, both substance use disorder and partner violence were significant predictors of engaging in commercial sex work. In their narrative responses, women frequently described how their addictions drove them to commercial sex work, often through the encouragement or coercion of violent men who played roles as dealers and pimps.

#43005 In her late 20s, she was having sex for money. It started when she ran out of money one night and the drug dealer made a proposal. Usually she had sex with the dealer….But she did start doing it with the Mexicans and everything. There was a lot of regret associated with that. She never got any diseases, just a lot of regret. It made her feel dirty and cheap.

#43031 She was physically beaten by pimps from age 17 on. If she went outside, she'd get her ass beat. If she'd mosey away from them and start to fall in love with someone that she tricked with, she'd get her ass beat. She wasn't allowed to have any feelings for customers. She wasn't allowed to have a cell phone. She wasn't allowed to communicate with anybody.

Figure 20. Interpolated Hazard at the Mean of Covariates for Onset of DUI/DUS

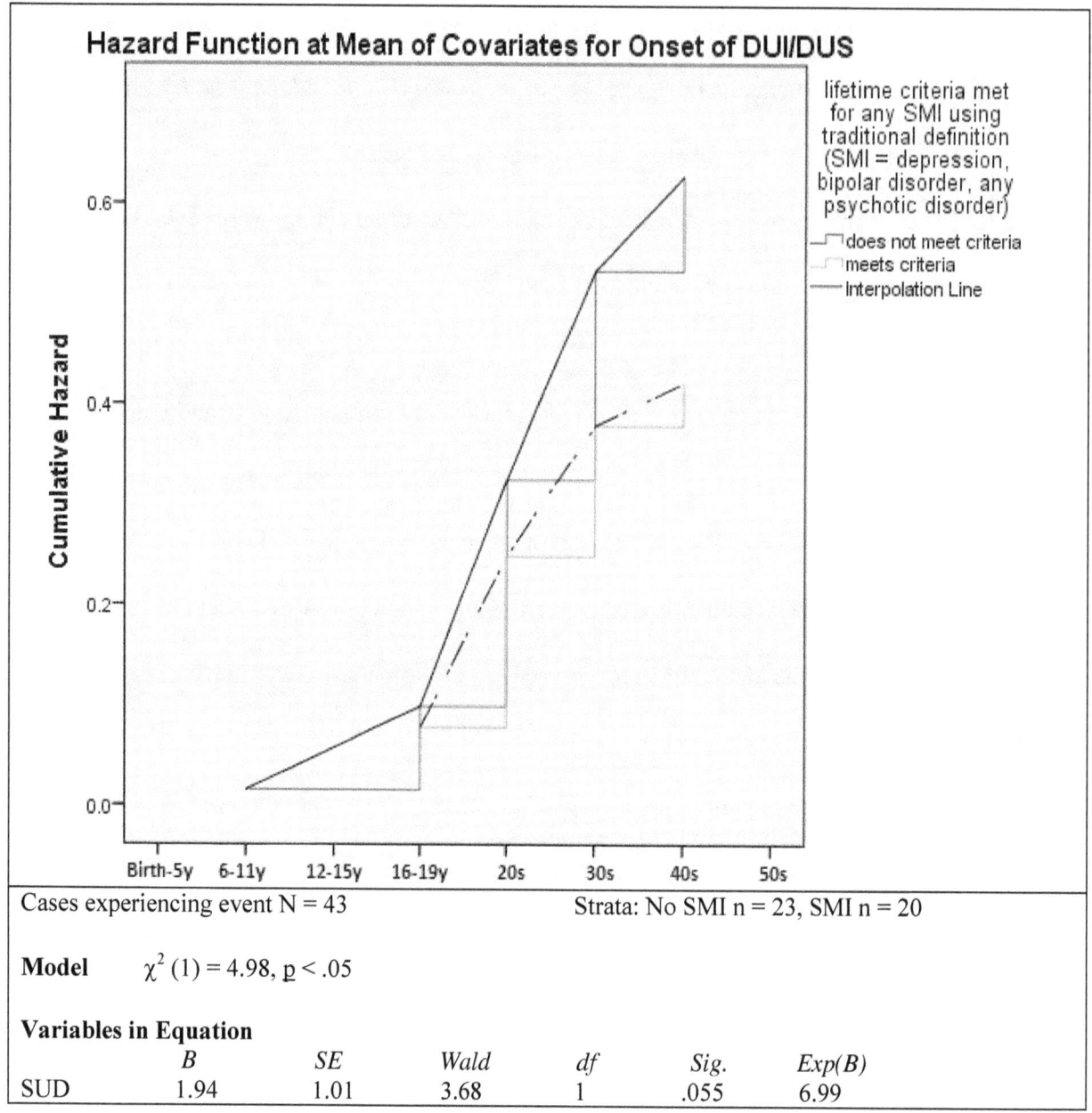

Cases experiencing event N = 43   Strata: No SMI n = 23, SMI n = 20

Model $\chi^2 (1) = 4.98, \underline{p} < .05$

Variables in Equation

	B	SE	Wald	df	Sig.	Exp(B)
SUD	1.94	1.01	3.68	1	.055	6.99

Figure 21. Interpolated Hazard at the Mean of Covariates for Onset of Sex Work

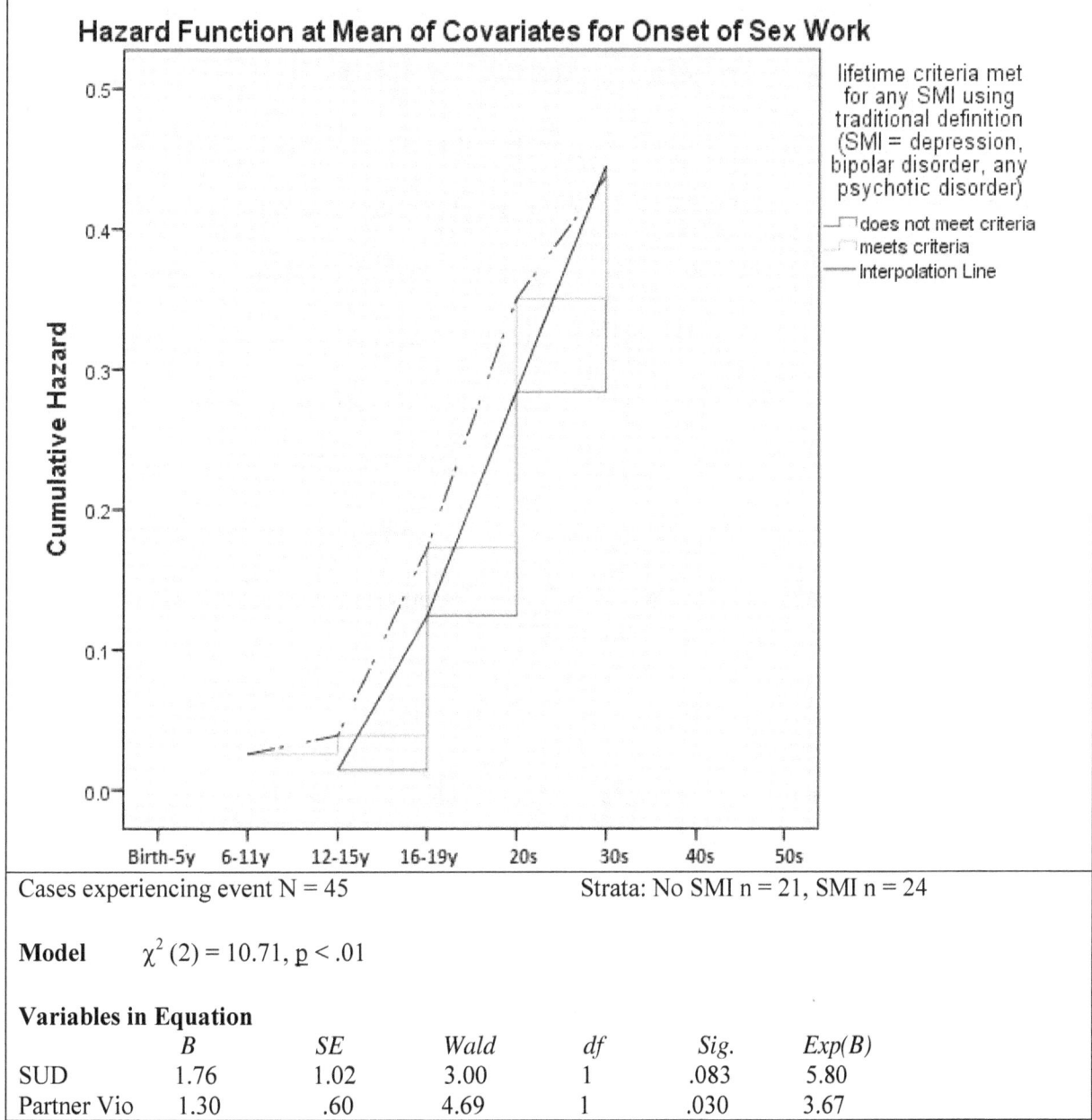

Cases experiencing event N = 45   Strata: No SMI n = 21, SMI n = 24

Model $\chi^2 (2) = 10.71, \underline{p} < .01$

Variables in Equation

	B	SE	Wald	df	Sig.	Exp(B)
SUD	1.76	1.02	3.00	1	.083	5.80
Partner Vio	1.30	.60	4.69	1	.030	3.67

The hazard ratios indicate that women with substance use disorder (SUD) were nearly six times as likely to engage in sex work relative to those who did not meet SUD diagnostic criteria, and women who experienced intimate partner violence were almost four times as likely to engage in sex work as those who did not experience partner violence.

Summary of regression findings.

Table 13 summarizes significant findings across these different Cox regression analyses. For ease of interpretation, we have sorted the table to group offenses with similar predictors. As illustrated in the table, substance use disorder was a significant contributor to risk for onset of substance use, driving under the influence, and commercial sex work. Intimate partner violence contributed to risk for commercial sex work and drug dealing/charges. Witnessing violence contributed to risk for property offenses, fighting/assault, and using weapons. Finally, caregiver violence contributed to risk for running away. Our stratification variable, SMI, demonstrated significant effects or trends in risk for substance use, drug dealing/charges, property crime, fighting/assault, and running away. The covariates PTSD, non-familial violence, sexual violence, and childhood non-victimization adversity did not meet criteria for entry into any of the Cox regression models.

Table 13

Significant Predictors of Substance Use and Crime Onset based on Cox Regression

Dependent variables	Significant predictors				Strata
Substance use				SUD	SMI
Driving under influence				SUD	
Commercial sex work			Partner Vio	SUD	
Drug dealing/charges			Partner Vio		SMI
Property crime		Witnessing Vio			SMI (trend)
Fighting/assault		Witnessing Vio			SMI (trend)
Weapons use/offenses		Witnessing Vio			
Running away	CG Violence				SMI

Part III: Staff Interviews

Methods

Participants

A total of 37 staff from the nine participating jails across the four sites took part in individual interviews or focus groups. Participants included a wide variety of correctional staff including correctional officers/deputy sheriffs, sergeants, captains, nurses, psychologists, psychiatrists, and social workers. Table 14 provides more specific demographic information about the staff member participants. Staff participants did not always choose to provide all of the demographic information, and in focus groups, more limited demographic information was collected.

About three-fifths (62%) of the staff sample were female, and two-thirds (67%) of the staff sample was White, a quarter Black/African American (25.5%), 6% Latino/a, and one staff member was Asian American. Almost half of the staff participants were supervisors (46%), such as sergeants, lieutenants, and captains. The staff participants ranged in age from 19 to 62 years old (avg. = 43) and with experience ranging from one-third of a year to 33 years with an average of 12 years of experience. In sum, this sample represented a variety of jobs within the jail, and included a range of years of experience, with roughly a third of the participants with five or fewer years of experience and a third with 15 or more years of experience.

Measures

All staff interviews and focus groups utilized prompts developed by project investigators for this study. Interview content included items asking staff to describe their thoughts about what leads women to jail, the overall mental health status of the women, whether women's trauma/violence experiences are related to the types of crimes they commit, differences between

Table 14

Staff Participant Demographics

Characteristic	N	%	(*n*)
Sex/Gender	37		
Female		62.2	(23)
Male		37.8	(14)
Race	36		
White		66.7	(24)
Black/Afr. American		25.0	(9)
Latino/a		5.6	(2)
Asian American		2.8	(1)
Job[1]	37		
Deputy/Corr. Officer		16.2	(6)
Health Provider		27.0	(10)
Supervisor		45.9	(17)
Other		10.8	(4)
Age[2]	24		
19-34		25.0	(6)
35-49		33.3	(8)
50-62		41.7	(10)
Years of Experience	23		
5 or fewer		34.8	(8)
6-14		26.1	(6)
15+		34.8	(8)
Jail Site	37		
Colorado		21.6	(8)
Idaho		24.3	(9)
South Carolina		32.4	(12)
Washington D.C.		21.6	(8)

[1]Healthcare providers were primarily psychologists, psychiatrists, and social workers, but also included nurses. The "other" category included a program coordinator, a training officer, and so on.

[2]Ages ranged from 19 to 62 years old, with an average of 43.3 years, a median of 44, and a mode of 50 years old.

[3]The years of experience ranged from 4 months to 33 years, with an average of 12.1 years, a median of 10 years, and a mode of 5 years.

women with and without SMI, the biggest risk factors leading women

back to jail after they are released, and the most critical needs of women both while incarcerated

in jail and for women re-entering their communities after leaving jail (See Appendix D).

Procedures

Staff members were interviewed either individually or in small groups in the jail

facilities. Participants were recruited by research team members or, in some cases, senior

corrections staff suggested good candidates for staff interviews. Thus, although all staff were

explicitly informed participation was voluntary and there would be no negative repercussions of

declining the interview, we are aware that staff participated for a variety of reasons (interest,

suggestion by a superior, availability). Staff did not receive any compensation for participating.

Staff members also likely responded differently depending on the format of the interview: a

small group versus one-on-one interviews. Thus, these findings should be taken as an additional

means of understanding women in jail, from those who work with them, with a goal of

identifying a broad range of beliefs and experiences rather than a summary of the *rates* at which

correctional staff adhere to risk factors for offending, re-offending, and so on, as our data do not

allow such reporting.

Finally, the staff interviews were transcribed into text documents. Then the data were

coded to look for major common themes.

Results

Below we describe the major themes that emerged in the individual and small group staff

interviews. These themes are not representative of the perspectives of all corrections staff but rather

demonstrate some common perceptions of corrections staff in a convenience sample (N = 37). To illustrate how these themes occurred within corrections staff members' narratives, we include quotations that are drawn from participants across the four sites and are identified by the staff member's role within the jail.

One commonly identified theme was staff participants' perception that trauma is a significant risk factor for women entering the criminal justice system. Staff typically listed several forms of trauma that they perceived to be linked with women's crimes. The most frequent references were to physical and sexual child abuse and neglect, but experiences of intimate partner violence in adolescent and adult dating relationships and violence from pimps were also often included.

> *(Mental Health Staff) [What leads women to jail?] Trauma across the board: physical, sexual, neglect and emotional. They are also victims of domestic violence. Just a lot of dysfunction and chaos in their upbringing. Lack of stability with relationships and housing.*

As is evident in the quotation above, staff members also observed that women were frequently raised in chaotic environments. They noted these environments were made more difficult by poverty and lack of support for obtaining education. In addition, another contributing factor to these chaotic environments was the offenders' family members' ongoing interactions with the criminal justice system. Several staff respondents noted that many women in jail are from families with multiple generations of criminal offending and incarceration. One deputy/correction officer spoke of a time when three generations of women (a grandmother, mother, and daughter) were all in the jail where she worked at the same time. Below is an additional example of a staff member observing the interactions among women's experiences of violence, early environment and lack of educational opportunities.

(Supervisor) Many of the inmates have a dysfunctional family, early trauma, molestation, rape, early introduction to illegal substances. . . Such a combination is a great recipe for being in jail. Dropping out of school is another huge problem.

A third theme raised in the staff interviews was the perception that women frequently have very low self-esteem, lack confidence, and low self-worth which staff members believed placed women at risk of making poor choices in partners and friends, and increased their likelihood of offending. Staff members appeared both compassionate and also at times frustrated as they described these observations.

(Supervisor) It all comes down to what a woman will do to have a man. These women are not sophisticated or refined, and they have low self-esteem. To get or keep a man, they will smoke crack, prostitute themselves, carry a gun, and commit robberies. This segues into them becoming criminals themselves. They start abusing drugs.

The next theme extracted revolved around staff members' perceptions that women's lack of resources places them at greater risk of both entering the system and also for re-offending and staying in the system.

(Mental Health Staff) Nine times out of ten they return because of probation or parole violations. Probation works great for people who have a job and family and can get to work and get around. Probation and parole are a set up for people who don't have access to money, transportation, a place to live. Even if you have a place to live, if you don't have the means to be transported to your probation meeting or pay for your UA, or pay to be supervised by your probation officer, which they have to do, it's a set up to fail.

(Deputy/Corrections Officer) And then they need a support group, family, friends - they need somewhere to live. Here it is "out the door you go" at release. I kind of feel bad. I don't know how you get a job without an address or someone to drive you to work until you get going, it's difficult to stay out of jail if you don't have anything.

Similarly, some staff perceived women to have little choice in regards to re-offending and returning to the system (e.g., "their life conditions made it impossible for them not to re-offend") whereas other staff indicated the belief women "could stop offending if they wanted to badly enough."

(Deputy/Corrections Officer) A lot of them know what they need to do, it's an issue of if they want to.

A number of staff members noted that the most significant need of women leaving jail is finding safe housing. Staff respondents talked about women having nowhere else to go but to return to abusive mates, abusive pimps, and/or neighborhoods fraught with drugs and violence. Some staff observed that these limited safe housing options were even more extreme for women with SMI, who had tested their family members' patience and resources, and could not even find a friend or relative's couch to stay on temporarily when they were released from jail.

(Supervisor) They need to a secure safe roof over their head. If not, they search for one and they end up with dealers, back in the situation with violence. They have to have a safe place to go, they need more shelters or programs.

(Supervisor) They may just not be able to cope when they are on the outside; they may not have a supportive family and so not have any place to go.

In addition to noting the specific need for housing, staff participants frequently observed that women have multiple needs for additional resources and supports when they are released, but that the available support is quite limited. Staff respondents identified needs including access to medications (particularly for women with SMI), child care, drug/alcohol free environments, jobs/job training, and educational programming.

> *(Supervisor) The jail doesn't have any long-term resources to address the mental health needs of these women.*

> *(Supervisor) Women need access to information about where they can go and what options they have. They may not have access to internet or libraries. Women would benefit from re-entry programs to help them get into shelters, get medication and drug treatment before they leave.*

The next identified theme from the staff interviews was staff awareness that the SMI rates among both jailed men and women have risen over the years as jails and prisons have become holding tanks for individuals with SMI and the community agencies that previously provided services became less available.

> *(Deputy/Corrections Officer) I noticed a rise in problems since we cut mental health services. . . . I don't think funding is there for services, so they come back ... it's easier to get illegal drugs then prescription drugs, the free care clinic closed...*

In their discussions about the lack of resources for individuals with SMI, some staff respondents also noted that sometimes individuals commit crimes to get arrested- for food and shelter-- and sometimes officers make an arrest so someone will get food and shelter.

The next common theme to emerge from the staff interviews was the idea that offenders' experiences of trauma, SMI, and offending are complicated and result in challenging treatment needs. Here the staff respondents discussed how inmates often could not be lumped together because they come with such different life experiences. Some staff members struggled with

63

chicken-egg types of concerns about what comes first: the mental illness, the trauma, the substance use/addiction, or the other offending (in addition to or instead of substance use). Additionally, staff members wondered how these events affect each other, and about the implications for the need to individualize treatment programs.

> *(Supervisor) The drugs and mental illness play on each other. The women may have mental health problems, then that's doubled once they start doing drugs, and that mix leads to criminal offenses. It's a rough cocktail.*

> *(Supervisor) Sometimes trauma can be linked with crimes as they learn a behavior (as victims) and then they become the aggressor, or they turn to drugs as an escape from their traumas or related symptoms, and drugs lead them to commit crimes.*

The final theme that emerged from the staff interviews related to differences between male and female offenders. Several staff members described the observation that women in jail are far more likely and willing to want to talk about their problems, including traumas and SMI, than their male counterparts. Most of these reports identified jailed women as being more relational and more open than jailed men, and most of the staff reported this gender difference as one that made it easier to identify and treat women's needs relative to the men in jail. Although in some cases, women's wish to discuss their problems was seen as a short-coming and an indication of "neediness."

(Supervisor) The non-clinical staff sees mental illness in women less and more in men, particularly chronic mental illness. The women are much more likely to tell you about it and to whine about it, and to want attention and feedback from correctional staff.

DISCUSSION

Our national sample of women in jails demonstrated high rates of mental health problems, with a majority of our participants meeting diagnostic criteria for serious mental illness, lifetime post-traumatic stress disorder, and/or substance use disorder. Interestingly, there were not differences in the rates of SMI, PSTD or SUD in urban versus rural locations although there were some significant regional differences with participants in the western regions reporting higher overall rates. This pattern of regional differences is similar to differences identified in a recent report of state by state comparisons of SMI (SAMHSA, 2011).

Similar to Steadman and colleagues' (2009) finding that 31% of female offenders residing in northeastern jails met criteria for a current SMI, 32% of participants in this multi-site study met criteria for a SMI in the past year. Further, much like Trestman and colleagues (2007) report that 56% of a large sample of females in jail experienced multiple lifetime disorders, in this multi-site study that assessed a more limited range of disorders (SMI, PTSD and SUD), 46% of the sample met criteria for lifetime PTSD and SUD while about one in three met criteria for lifetime SMI and SUD, and about one in five met criteria for SMI, PSTD, and SUD in their lifetime. Perhaps most critical to consider to gauge the treatment needs of female offenders at the time of incarceration, 20% met criteria for current SMI and SUD, 14% of participants met criteria for both current SMI and PTSD, and almost one in ten met criteria for current SMI, PTSD, and SUD. These rates suggest female offenders enter (or re-enter) jail with substantial and often co-occurring mental health concerns, and subsequently, have complex treatment needs.

Although over half the sample had accessed treatment prior to incarceration, one in five disagreed that they had received quality mental health treatment in their most recent treatment experience, and one in three disagreed that their symptoms and functioning improved. Treatment quality and outcome was somewhat better for the most recent substance focused treatment, although one in four reported their symptoms and coping did not improve. In addition, from 30 to 45% of individuals with a current disorder reported severely impaired functioning associated with SMI, PSTD or SUD in the past year. Thus, a significant portion of female offenders do not appear to have access to treatment that is addressing their problems and helping them to improve their basic level of functioning. These levels of reported impairment combined with the frequency of SMI, PTSD, and SUD rates in this population suggest the critical need for additional resources for mental health assessment and treatment with this population.

The victimization rates identified in this study are similar to those reported by incarcerated women and girls in prior studies (Belknap & Holsinger, 2006; DeHart, 2009; Green et al, 2005; Lynch et al, 2012). Further, given the evidence from the general literature of elevated risk for increased psychological distress/disorders after experiences of chronic or multiple traumatic events (e.g., polyvictimization, Hedtke et al., 2008; Turner, Finklehor & Ormrod, 2005), it is not surprising that women with SMI reported significantly greater frequency of all forms of victimization. In general, the findings from the structural equation model analyses supported existing research on the link between victimization and mental health as women's experiences of child and adult trauma were significant predictors of their overall mental health difficulties. In addition, experiences of re-victimization as an adult mediated the relationship between child victimization and mental health. Thus, experiencing victimization as an adult, subsequent to childhood victimization increased risk of poorer mental health. Most importantly, however, was the finding that although more extensive victimization was directly associated with greater mental health problems, victimization experiences did not directly predict offending. Instead, women's mental health mediated the relationship between victimization and offending such that women with more victimization had poorer mental health, and poorer mental health predicted offending histories. Several studies have identified an association between victimization and offending (Grella, Stein, & Greenwell, 2005; Widom, 2000; see also DeHart & Lynch, 2012 for a review). The findings of this study offer potential insight or explanation for this link, suggesting one way that victimization influences offending behaviors is via mental health problems. These findings also suggest that implementing interventions for at-risk girls and incarcerated women that address trauma-related distress and mental health problems may decrease entry or re-entry into the system.

Analyses utilizing the data provided via the in-depth Life History Calendar interviews demonstrate how SMI is associated with increased risk of *onset* of a number of offending behaviors and how this is exacerbated by experiences of victimization and drug use. Women with SMI were at higher risk across the lifespan for onset of numerous forms of offending including running away, substance use and drug dealing/charges. In addition, substance use disorders specifically were related to earlier onset of substance use, driving under the influence, and commercial sex work.

In addition to the increased risk associated with SMI, various forms of traumatic victimization predicted the onset of offending. Experiences of intimate partner violence were a factor in women's drug offending and commercial sex work. This seemed to relate to intimate involvement with violent men who vacillated between roles as the women's co-offenders, drug dealers, and pimps. Next, witnessing violence was associated with women's onset of engaging in property crimes, fighting, and use of weapons. Sometimes this stemmed from affiliation with criminal networks, and often women's use of weapons or aggression appeared to arise from efforts to protect themselves or others. One of the strongest associations was between experiences of caregiver violence and running away as a teen. This finding supports a growing body of evidence that runaway youth often enact this behavior as a means of escaping intolerable maltreatment at home.

The potential impact of this project is multifold. First, existing studies (e.g., Trestman et al., 2007) note that many offenders with SMI are not identified as mentally ill upon entry into the system. Given that mental health problems in offenders are linked to greater likelihood of violent crimes, longer sentences, rule violations, and physical assaults in the corrections environment (Felson, Silver & Remster, 2012; James & Glaze, 2006), greater knowledge and understanding of these offenders and their needs is critical for the success of behavioral health treatment programs, jail management, and correctional staff safety. Understanding female offenders' pathways to offending helps elucidate the complexity of their experiences and identify key factors and intervening variables that may ameliorate or exacerbate risk. This type of research is critical to development of gender responsive programming (Hills et al., 2004), trauma informed mental health treatment, alternatives to incarceration, and problem-solving court initiatives. Women's trauma and mental health histories, gender-specific ways of coping, and pivotal life experiences are important components of informing justice practice at the federal, state, and local level to develop effective contexts for intervention. Findings are important for professionals working not only in juvenile and adult investigation, courts, and corrections, but also those in child welfare and youth services, substance abuse and rehabilitation services, housing and employment services, and services for persons with special needs.

Recommendations

Investigators met with stakeholders to share the findings from this study and to solicit suggestions about how this information might be most useful to the corrections community and professionals intersecting with juvenile and adult female offenders. Stakeholders included sheriffs, jail captains, corrections and detention officers, mental health staff in jails, professionals associated with community mental health or support programs (e.g., housing), professionals involved with mental health court, attorneys, and probation and detention officers working with juvenile offenders. Feedback from the staff interviews are also incorporated into this list of recommendations.

The prevalence rates of the women's mental health problems and victimization experiences generally did not surprise the stakeholders with whom we shared these results. Many expressed appreciation that a study had been conducted that seemed to validate their observations from the field. In discussions after we shared the results, stakeholders across the sites shared the following observations, concerns and recommendations:

1. One of the most consistently identified needs was for programming and support services post release from jail to provide a continuum of care (including access to medication and mental health treatment). Specifically, professionals working with adults and youths identified the need for service coordination and for clearly established best practice guidelines for professionals assisting juvenile and adult offenders in developing and carrying out after care plans.

   A. In some regions, corrections staff noted the absence of a corrections – community partnership to facilitate service coordination while other regions appeared to have established communication.

   B. Some stakeholders noted that staff in jails experience greater uncertainty about the length of offenders' stays or when they will be released as compared to staff working with offenders in prison. They indicated this makes it challenging to coordinate or plan for after care.

2. For adults, stakeholders and corrections staff frequently identified the need for safe transitional housing as a significant, needed component of after care support. Many staff and professionals commented on the lack of transitional housing and noted women frequently have no where to go other than back to the environment where they committed their crime(s) and where they are at risk of further victimization.

3. Another need identified by corrections staff in interviews and by stakeholders in feedback sessions was for better alternatives to incarceration.

   A. One example raised by different stake holders was the barriers for female offenders participating in mental health courts. Stakeholders including probation officers and attorneys noted that limited capacity, lengthier time to completion and increased cost (e.g., paying for classes/programs) of mental health courts as compared to serving jail time frequently prevented offenders from applying for this alternative to incarceration.

   B. Similarly, corrections staff noted the absence of community detox centers or community agencies for the mentally ill that resulted in increased incarceration rates as there was no where else to take these individuals. Many identified community interest in but insufficient funds for these types of facilities.

4. Many stakeholders also noted the limited resources of most jails for mental health care provision and the need for additional resources for both screening individuals and providing services developed to address women's complex mental health needs during incarceration.

   A. Staff members' varied in regards to their knowledge of programming available to address co-occurring disorders. Some staff were highly cognizant of existing programs and even had funding allocated for treatment but noted that the funding was often for specific problems (e.g., substance use) which restricted their ability to use it to address multiple concerns simultaneously.

5. Given limited resources, stakeholders recognized the importance of disseminating findings of this study to individuals making funding decisions. For example, it became clear that for several jails, it would be essential to educate county commissioners about the prevalence of mental health problems in female inmates as they are often the funding decision makers for jails.

6. A variety of stakeholders indicated that short fact sheets and brief descriptions of study findings (e.g., a brief write up that could be included in various agency or organizational newsletters) had the greatest utility for dissemination and training purposes. Some sites suggested that community presentations were critical to gaining buy in from funding decision makers.

> A. Staff who were supervisors generally indicated this information would be useful to provide during trainings to corrections or detention officers, but a number of corrections officers indicated their belief they had sufficient training in regards to mental health concerns in inmates (particularly focused on recognizing suicidal ideation or utilizing restraints).

References

Axinn, W., Pearce, L., & Ghimire, D. (1999). Innovations in Life History Calendar applications. *Social Science Research, 28,* 243-264.

Belknap, J. & Holsinger, K. (2006). The gendered nature of risk factors for delinquency. *Feminist Criminology,1*(1), 48-71.

Belli, R. (1998). The structure of autobiographical memory and the event history calendar: Potential improvements in the quality of retrospective reports in surveys. *Memory, 6,* 383-406.

Bentler, P. M. (1990). Fit indexes, Lagrange multipliers, constraint changes and incomplete data in structural models. *Multivariate Behavioral Research, 25,* 169-172.

Bentler, P. M., & Bonnett, D. G. (1980). Significance tests and goodness of fit in the analysis of covariance structures. *Psychological Bulletin, 88,* 588-606.

Browne, A., Miller, B., & Maguin, E. (1999). Prevalence and severity of lifetime physical and sexual victimization among incarcerated women. *International Journal of Law & Psychiatry, 22,* 301-322.

Carlson, B., & Shafer, M. (2010). Traumatic histories and stressful life events of incarcerated parents: Childhood and adult trauma histories. *The Prison Journal, 90(4),* 475-493.

Center for Mental Health Services. *Mental Health, United States, 2004.* Manderscheid, R.W., and Berry, J.T., eds. DHHS Pub no. (SMA)-06-4195. Rockville, MD: Substance Abuse and Mental Health Services Administration, 2006.

DeHart, D.D. (2008). Pathways to prison: Impact of victimization in the lives of incarcerated women. *Violence Against Women,* 14(12), 1362-1381.

DeHart, D. D. (2009). *Polyvictimization among Girls in the Juvenile Justice System: Manifestations and Associations to Delinquency.* Washington, DC: USDOJ, NCJ#228620.

DeHart, D.D. & Lynch, S. M. (2012). Victimization and offending. In C. Renzetti, S. Miller & A. Gover (Eds.) *Routledge International Handbook of Gender and Crime Studies.* New York, NY: Routledge Publishing.

DeHart, D. D., & Moran, R. (in press). Poly-victimization among girls in the justice system: Trajectories of risk and associations to juvenile offending. *Violence Against Women.*

Diamond, P. M., Wang, E.W., Holzer, C.E., Thomas, C. Cruser, A (2001). The prevalence of mental illness in prison. *Administration and Policy in Mental Health, 29,* 21-40.

Felitti, V., & Anda, R. (2009). The relationship of adverse childhood experiences to adult medical disease, psychiatric disorders, and sexual behavior: Implications for healthcare. In R. Lanius & E. Vermetten (Eds.) *The Hidden Epidemic: The Impact of Early Life Trauma on Health and Disease.* Cambridge University Press.

Felson, R.B., Silver, E., & Remster, B. (2012) Mental disorder and offending in prison. *Criminal Justice and Behavior, 39,* 125-143.

Finkelhor, D., Ormrod, R., Turner, H., & Hamby, S. (2005). Measuring poly-victimization using the Juvenile Victimization Questionnaire. *Child Abuse & Neglect, 29,* 1297-1312.

Freedman, D., Thornton, A., Camburn, D., Alwin, D., & Young-DeMarco, L. (1988). The life history calendar: A technique for collecting retrospective data. *Sociological Methodology, 18,* 37-68.

Green, B.L., Miranda, J., Daroowalla, A., & Siddique, J. (2005). Trauma exposure, mental health functioning and program needs of women in jail. *Crime and Delinquency, 51,* 133-151.

Grella, C.E., Stein, J.A., & Greenwell, L. (2005). Associations among childhood trauma, adolescent behavior problems, and adverse adult outcomes in substance-abusing women offenders. *Psychology of Addictive Behaviors, 19,* 43-53.

Hamby, S., & Finkelhor, D. (2004). *The comprehensive Juvenile Victimization Questionnaire.* Durham, NH: Crimes against Children Research Center.

Hedtke, K.A., Ruggiero, K.J., Fitzgerald, M.M, Zinzow, H.M., Saunders, B.E., Resnick, H.S., Kilpatrick, D.G. (2008). A longitudinal investigation of interpersonal violence in relation to mental health and substance use. *Journal of Consulting & Clinical Psychology*, 76 (4), 633-647.

Hills, H., Siegfried, C., & Ickowitz, A. (2004). *Effective Prison Mental Health Services: Guidelines to Expand and Improve Treatment.* Washington D.C.: U.S. Department of Justice.

Hu, L. & Bentler, P. M. (1999) Cutoff criteria for fit indexes in covariance structure analysis: Conventional criteria versus...*Structural Equation Modeling, 6,* 1-50.

James, D., & Glaze, L. (2006). Mental health problems of prison and jail inmates. Bureau of Justice Statistics Special Report. Washington, DC: United States Department of Justice.

Lynch, S., Fritch, A., & Heath, N. (2012). Looking beneath the surface: The nature of incarcerated women's experiences of interpersonal violence, treatment needs, and mental health. *Feminist Criminology, 7,* 381-400.

MacKinnon, D. (2008). *Introduction to Statistical Mediation Analysis. New York:* Taylor & Francis Group.

MacKinnon, D. Lockwood, C., Hoffman, J., West, S. & Sheets, V. (2002) A comparison of methods to test mediation and other intervening variable effects. *Psychological Methods, 7,* 83-104.

MacKinnon, D., Fairchild, A. & Fritz, M. (2007). Mediation analysis. *Annual Reviewof Psychology, 58,* 593-614.

Minton, T. D. (2012). Jail inmates at midyear 2011—Statistical tables. Washington, DC: United States Department of Justice.

Schumacker, R. E., & Lomax, R. G. (2010). *A beginner's guide to structural equation modeling* (3rd ed.). New York: Routledge Academic.

Singer, J., & Willett, J. (1991). Modeling the days of our lives: Using survival analysis when designing and analyzing longitudinal studies of duration and the time of events. *Psychological Bulletin, 110(2),* 268-290.

Sobel, M. E. (1982). Asymptotic intervals for indirect effects in structural equations models. In S. Leinhart (Ed.), *Sociological methodology 1982* (pp.290-312). San Francisco: Jossey-Bass.

Steadman H.J., Osher F.C., Robbins P.C., Case B., Samuels S. (2009). Prevalence of serious mental illness among jail inmates. *Psychiatric Services, 60* (6), 761-5.

Steiger, J. H., & Lind, J. C. (1980). *Statistically based tests for the number of common factors.* Paper presented at the Annual Meeting of the Psychometric Society, Iowa City, IA.

Substance Abuse and Mental Health Services Administration, Center for Behavioral Health

    Statistics and Quality. (October 6, 2011). *The NSDUH Report: State Estimates of Adult*

    Mental Illness. Rockville, MD.

Sutton, J. E. (2010). A review of the life-events calendar method for criminological research.

    Journal of Criminal Justice, 38, 1038-1044.

Sutton, J. E., Bellair, P. E., Kowalski, B. R., Light, R., & Hutcherson, D. (2011). Reliability and

    validity of prisoner self-reports gathered using the life event calendar method. *Journal of*

    Quantitative Criminology, 27, 151-171.

Trestman, R.L., Ford, J., Zhang, W. & Wiesbrock, V. (2007) Current and lifetime psychiatric

    illness among inmates not identified as acutely mentally ill at intake in Connecticut's

    jails. *Journal of the American Academy of Psychiatry and the Law, 35*(4), 490-500.

Tucker, L. R., & Lewis, C. (1973). The reliability coefficient for maximum likelihood factor

    analysis. *Psychometrika, 38(1),* 1-10.

Turner, H., Finkelhor, D., & Ormrod, R. (2006). The effect of lifetime victimization on the

    mental health of children and adolescents. *Social Science & Medicine*, 62, 13-27.

Widom, C.S. (2000). Childhood victimization and the derailment of girls and women to the

    criminal justice system. *Plenary Papers of the 1999 Conference on Criminal Justice*

    Research and Evaluation—Enhancing Policy and Practice Through Research, 3, 27-36.

Wolfe, J., & Kimerling, R. (1997). Gender issues in the assessment of Posttraumatic Stress

    Disorder. In J. Wilson & T.M. Keane (Eds.), Assessing psychological trauma and PTSD

    (pp. 192-238). New York: Guilford.

World Health Organization (1990). *Composite International Diagnostic Interview.* Geneva,

    Switzerland: WHO.

Appendices

Appendix A: Explanation of adaptations to assess for psychotic symptoms and disorders

In order to assess for the presence of psychotic disorders, as well as to distinguish between them (i.e., brief psychotic disorder, shizophreniform, schizophrenia, shizoaffective disorder, delusional disorder), adaptations to the Psychotic Screen for the CIDI were made. First, we split the CIDI Psychotic Screen into two parts. The first was a set of screening items that were administered with the CIDI General Screening and the second part became our Psychotic Module that was only administered subsequent to endorsement of psychotic symptoms in the screening. Items were added to each section in order to meet our goal of having a structured assessment of full DSM-IV criteria as well as differential diagnosis among the psychotic disorders. To the screen, we added items to assess delusional thinking (i.e., somatic delusions, delusions of grandeur, religious delusions) and added a final item to allow the interviewer to indicate having observed grossly inappropriate affect, disorganized speech, alogia (impoverishment in thinking that is observed from speech and language behavior), or affective flattening (blunted, limited, or complete lack of emotional expression). Additions to the second part of the CIDI, our Psychotic Module, consisted of a selected set of SCID Research Version Psychotic Module items that were adapted in order to enable a structured diagnostic interview of psychotic disturbance. The language of SCID items was adapted so as best to resemble and thus be consistent with the other CIDI items; we wanted the interview to seamlessly transition from one module to the next. Regarding content, the items selected and adapted from the SCID primarily functioned to assess the presence and degree of overlap between psychotic and mood symptoms, to rule out psychosis due to substance use or other psychiatric conditions, and to assess functional impairment attributed to each type of psychotic disturbance. Skip instructions and "Interviewer Checkpoints" were written to match the CIDI format and enable navigation through the module. In addition, treatment access and quality items equivalent to those added to the other CIDI modules were also developed for the psychotic module. After all items were drafted, a clinical psychologist and clinical graduate student compared the screen items and Psychotic Module, item by item, to the DSM-IV diagnostic criteria to ensure it the interview would gather sufficient information to arrive at an accurate diagnosis. Finally, the module was administered to student volunteers so that the wording of individual items could be pilot tested. Minor changes were made to wording to increase ease of administration and interpretation of items by research participants.

Appendix B: Treatment Quality and Outcome Items

The following items were excerpted from the 2004 Mental Health report published by the Substance Abuse and Mental Health Services Administration (SAMHSA). These items were included in each module.

Instructions adapted for structured interview:
Think about the most recent time you received treatment for _____ (disorder being assessed) before this current incarceration. Please rate how true the following statements are to describe your treatment experience where

Strongly Disagree   Strongly Agree
                1   2   3   4   5

Quality/Appropriateness of Treatment/Services
- When you needed services right away, you were able to see someone as soon as you wanted.
- The people you went to for services spent enough time with you.
- The people you went to for services were sensitive to your cultural background (race, religion, language, sexual orientation, etc.).
- You were given information about different services that were available to you.
- You were given enough information to effectively handle my condition.

Perceived Outcomes of Treatment/Services
- After receiving treatment at that time, your symptoms did not bother you as much.
- You were better able to cope when things go wrong.
- You were better able to accomplish the things you wanted to do.
- You were less likely to use alcohol and other drugs.
- You were doing better in work/school.

Appendix C:

Life History Calendar Method

Instructions adapted from the National Survey of Family Growth (2003). Cycle 6 Main Study Female Questionnaire. Hyattsville, MD: Centers for Disease Control, National Center for Health Statistics. Available at www.cdc.gov.

Calendar Introduction

"Many people we have talked to have found that having a calendar to look at helped them to remember when something happened to them. We will be talking about dates during the interview, and getting accurate dates is very important. At times I will ask you to enter specific events on the calendar. You may find it helps to mark other important events on the calendar as we go along. You may also find it helpful to make a line through several months or years to show a period of time, such as when you were in school or when you were working."

Calendar Demonstration

"Let's begin with the year you were born." [Interviewer asks year and, in clear view of the woman, writes as column heading and fills in subsequent years/ages up until the present].

"Now let's try using the calendar to mark a few events. I'd like you to think of two or three things that happened in your life that really stand out in your memory. These can be any events, such as getting your first bicycle, birth of a son or daughter, starting your first job, vacations, or anything else." [Interviewer marks and continues with memorable events until it is clear that the girl has a basic understanding of the calendar].

Calendar Purpose

"The events and times on the calendar should act as reminders to help you remember other dates later in the interview. Sometimes we'll be asking how old you were at some event in your life. You can use the calendar to help figure that out. Now let's continue with the interview.

SAMPLE LIFE HISTORY CALENDAR (actual sample from girl in DeHart, 2009 study)

Grade	Pre	1	2	3	4	5	6	7	8	9	10	11
School	As & Bs		Suspended & write-ups for disrespecting teachers, disturbing school, cigarettes, tardiness				Fs; fights in school					
Home	live w/Mom, Dad, Sis			Mom &Sis / Divorce	Dad, Stepmom, Grandmom			Mom / D drank more	Dad	Grandmom	Mom	M/SD crack
AOD	drinking some			smoking pot / huffing			drinking regularly	coke		meth		
Crime						Trespass / Dmg prop		Disturbing school / Drv w/o lic	Incite riot	Dirty urine / Drv w/o lic	Grand larc / Selling crack / Poss gun / Endanger child / Shoplifting, stealing / Prostitution	
Victimization	SA - cousin / SA - teen / SA - boys	Witn M/D phys fighting	SA - teen	D beat			D beat	D/SM call whore / SA - drug / Sex w/older men			Dating violence / Witness dope vio	M/SD beat

Appendix D: Prompts for corrections staff interview

Corrections/MH Staff Prompts

1. What are some of your ideas about what led these women to jail?
   - What types of problems did they have in their lives?
   - How do you think their life situations influenced their decisions?

2. How would you describe the overall mental health status of women in this jail?
   - How are the mental health issues for women in here different than those of the men?
   - How do you work differently with the women around mental health?

3. What type of connections do you see between women's experiences of violence or trauma and the crimes they've done?
   - How are the trauma histories for women in here are different than those of the men?
   - Does this make a difference in how you work with the women (compared to the men)?

4. Do you see differences in the life experiences of women with and without serious mental illness?
   - To what extent do inmates with SMI have needs that are different from other offenders?
   - Do you work differently with women with mental illness versus other female offenders?

5. When the women in here get released, what's the biggest danger in terms of things that might lead them back to jail?
   - What will they need to make it through--what do you see in success stories?

6. What do you see as the most critical needs of female offenders in jail?
   - What training do correctional staff have or need to respond to these offenders (COs, MH staff)?
   - What types of programs (corrections or transition) could help women in jail the most?

7. What do you see as the most critical needs of female offenders getting out of jail/re-entry?
   - What training do correctional staff have or need to respond to these offenders (COs, MH staff)?
   - What types of programs (corrections or transition) could help women get out and stay out?

8. Other thoughts about what is necessary for successful rehabilitation of female offenders?